ARE WE THERE YET?

The Journey to a Dependent Relationship with God

BILL KASPER

www.overcominglaodicea.org

ARE WE THERE YET?

The Journey to a Dependent Relationship with God

BiLL KASPER

ISBN-13: 979-8-5591-3448-2

ISBN-10: 8-5591-3448-2

CONTENTS

INTRODUCTION

BACK SEAT LESSONS

RE WE THERE YET? If you have ever taken a trip with children, you have very likely heard this question. It doesn't matter how long the trip will take either. You could be on an eight-day road excursion across the country or an eight-minute dash to the grocery store. This question might even be asked before the car leaves the driveway. Of course, some children ask for no other reason than boredom, but most children ask because time is different for them than for adults—they have a difficult time judging how long *any* trip will take.

I remember sitting in the back seat of my parents' car on many trips—journeys both long and short. We didn't have cell phones or video devices to occupy our time, so I would often just stare out the window watching the scenery pass by. Whenever we were going somewhere exciting, like an amusement park or Grandma's house, I couldn't wait to arrive and would always wonder how much time was left on our journey. My curiosity was usually vocalized with that famous question. I couldn't help it! Time was distorted in the car. *Every* trip felt long to me. The anticipation was unbearable.

I know I'm not alone in this. Whenever we begin a journey to a desirable place, we want to get there as quickly as possible. If we are not in control of the direction or speed of travel, time tends to crawl. In my experience, it is even worse the first time I go somewhere—it invariably feels longer, especially if I am just a passenger in the back seat.

Sometimes it can feel like we are in the back seat on the Christian journey. Arriving at the ultimate destination—a trusting, personal relationship with God—can feel like the longest road trip ever. Maybe you've been on this journey before (you may still be traveling). You felt the Holy Spirit convicting you, which resulted in giving your heart to God. You experienced the burden of guilt lifted as you accepted God's forgiveness. In the beginning, each day was fresh and exciting. You were making great progress. However, a fulfilling relationship with God still feels a long way off.

Fortunately, there's a story in the Old Testament that parallels our journey with God. It is the story of the Israelites, specifically, the account of their exodus from Egypt and their ensuing journey to the Promised Land. Most often, we look at the Promised Land as a symbol of Heaven. While it has some similarities, the land of Canaan represents something even greater: it's the place where God is King. This place will ultimately be Heaven, but it can also exist here on earth. In other words, we do not have to wait until we get to heaven to have God as our King.

Every follower of God begins at the same place as the Israelites: slavery. We may not be slaves to a foreign nation, but we are all slaves to sin. Their exodus from Egypt is similar to the moment we first accept Jesus as our Savior—it is the moment we are *set free* from the bondage of sin. Many Christians have the misbelief that the moment we are liberated we will automatically trust God. The truth is, learning to fully trust God is a journey. The

Israelites left Egypt with a "relationship" with God, but it was shallow—they knew *of* Him but didn't really trust Him. They needed more time with God for their relationship with Him to become fully dependent. Thus, the journey. A journey that, for us, can feel long.

In this book, we will travel with the Israelites on their trip to the Promised Land. We will join them as they leave Egypt with the promise of a better life. We will experience detours and dead ends with them. We will experience tests and miracles. We will meet God at His mountain and face some important choices. Through the wilderness and into the land of Canaan, all along the way, we will glean lessons that parallel our own journey to a dependent relationship with God.

There are many lessons we can learn from their experiences—their obstacles and challenges, as well as how God carried them through. However, it is beyond the scope of this book to look at every incident Israel encountered or every lesson they learned during the many years with God in the wilderness. Nor can we cover every possible scenario we might face as we walk with God. Instead, we will focus on a few major moments in their story that have a significant impact on us throughout our spiritual journey. Those moments will help explain what is needed to make it to, and thrive in, the land where God is King. They will also reveal why that destination can feel so far away.

That is what this book is about: understanding the journey to a dependent relationship with God. Over the upcoming pages, we will travel with Israel from slavery (in sin) to the land of freedom (having God as the true King of our lives).

Our bags are packed, and our tickets are in hand. We are now ready to begin our journey. Find a comfortable seat, buckle up, and let's go!

"The Lord is not slow to fulfill his promise as some count slowness, but is patient toward you, not wishing that any should perish, but that all should reach repentance"

2 PETER 3:9

CHAPTER 1

UNDERSTANDING THE DETOUR

It was supposed to be an uneventful pick-up at the airport. My wife and I had taken the trip many times and knew exactly how long it would take. We were driving from a city in the southwestern corner of Michigan to the Chicago O'Hare airport—about a three-hour drive. It was anything but uneventful though. About half way through the trip we found ourselves in a traffic jam due to construction. The traffic was barely moving (a glacier could have passed us). After having traveled only about a quarter of a mile in forty-five minutes, an idea popped into my mind: I would take the next exit, not far from where we were, and access another road in order to bypass the traffic.

I turned onto the ramp of the next exit and we enjoyed blissful speed-limit traffic . . . for about a half a mile. After that short duration, we found ourselves at the end of *another* traffic jam, due *again* to construction. We waited for awhile in that snail-paced line when the same idea reentered my mind. I'd take the next exit off *that* road and take a different road around the new situation (you'd think I would have learned already). So, when the next exit appeared, I took it.

We traveled a few back roads and found ourselves further from our intended path—entering into increasingly run-down residential areas of Chicago. It wasn't long before we realized that we had no idea where we were (this was before we had GPS on our phones). We were, eventually, able to find our way to a major highway and then to the airport. Unfortunately, due to the detours, our three-hour trip took over six hours—forcing my mother-in-law to wait at the airport for more than three hours, having no idea where we were!

I don't know very many people who enjoy an unplanned detour. Sure, there are times that you plan to take the road "less traveled," or an unexpected change of route takes you on a more scenic drive. But most detours happen when you know where you want to go and you want to get there as quickly as possible, but you get sidetracked. It's the kind of trip you faithfully research, Googling the best route and double-checking it on a map (okay, this may be a bit old-school), only to run into a "situation" on your way. These are the detours that send you *far* out of your way, down obscure roads—some that may not have seen a car in decades—basically making you lost. The detours that take you so far off the beaten path that even the GPS has no idea where you are. It is during such situations that you might find yourself, after you have followed the first detour sign, beginning to wonder if you missed the second sign that would bring you back to your intended route.

This can happen often in life. Not just while taking a family trip, but in other areas of life as well. You can experience detours in the pursuit of a career, or furthering your education, or on the journey to financial freedom. Instead of going the straightest, quickest way possible, you end up taking what appears to be the longest way around. Such detours can be extremely frustrating.

Furthermore, regardless of how beneficial a detour may be, most are usually viewed negatively. Even if an important detour, like re-routing around an accident or avoiding a bridge that is out, keeps us from reaching our goals in the quickest way possible, it is not good. Of course, some detours are of our own doing, and others we are led into.

Sadly, this is also true in our Christian experience. In fact, we often believe we have more detours in life than anyone else! It seems like no matter how hard we try to live "by faith"—devoting our lives to follow only Christ—there's usually a "detour" waiting, making our journey go way off course. It sometimes appears as though, once we become excited or passionate about something—like Jesus' second coming—it is farther away than ever. As a result, it often feels like God Himself is slow. It can seem like He's taking us the long way. Have you ever experienced this?

I believe the best way to understand the spiritual detours in which we may find ourselves is to look at one of the largest detours in Biblical history. It's the story of Israel, recorded in the book of Exodus. Fortunately, we've been invited to share the back seat with the Children of Israel on the greatest road trip ever: from Egypt to the Promised Land. It's the incredible journey from slavery in Egypt to freedom in the land where God is King.

I would offer again, though, that this story in Exodus is not simply a history lesson about the Israelites and how they entered into Canaan, but is also a parallel to our Christian journey. Jesus told us that we can experience God as our King right here on earth (Mark 1:15)—we don't have to wait until heaven. So while the Promised Land is often used to represent Heaven, it is more notable as a symbol of the Lordship of God in our lives. This is our true destination. In fact, Heaven isn't Heaven without God as our King. Therefore, every one of us will go on, or is already on, this journey: from slavery and death in sin to complete faith in God as King of our lives. Maybe you've already finished this trip and have reached the destination of full dependence on God. If so, praise the Lord! Don't look back. But it is also possible that you are just about to start this journey, or are somewhere in between—you don't want to live in sin anymore, but you do not fully trust in God. Regardless of where we may be on the journey, it is to our benefit to ride along with Israel, because we'll be able to pick up some traveling tips for our own journey with God.

Before we board the Promised Land charter bus with the Israelites, though, we should meet them. Their story starts a little before Exodus 13. Without going into a long history lesson, this group is made up of the descendants of Jacob. Originally, their ancestors moved to Egypt during the time of Joseph and had, by the time of the Exodus, lived there for 430 years—mostly as slaves. Then, not long before they began this massive journey, they were promised (by an ex-murderer renegade) freedom, their own country, and a better life. This would have been really good news —a Gospel, if you will—to them. It was almost *too* good to be true. Their freedom from Egypt would not be cheap though. It would happen only after terrible plagues and miraculous events. As you can imagine, on the day they left, they were more than ready!

In addition to being set free, the Lord gave the Children of Israel favor in the eyes of the Egyptians—to the extent that they gave the Israelites whatever they asked for (Exodus 12:33–36). The Egyptians *urged* them to leave. As a result, the Israelites plundered the Egyptians! What an interesting turn of events. After so many years of slavery, they were finally free and had the opportunity to take from the people who had enslaved them without a battle or long negotiations—*they just asked*. They ended up leaving Egypt with everything they would need for the journey.

How amazing is this? When God frees us from the slavery of sin, He does not expect us to leave that life empty handed. Yes, we will leave behind the oppression and emptiness in which our former life held us. However, we will bring from our experience things that will help us along the way. In a way, you could say that when we are freed from sin, we plunder Satan. Great musical talent that could have been used for indulging selfish and destructive goals will be plundered from the enemy and used to glorify God with humility and grace. Natural leadership skills and charismatic personalities that might have been misused to deceive and steal will be plundered and used to break down Satan's strongholds and empower people to follow God. Passion and energy that would otherwise be used to satisfy one's own appetites and desires will be plundered from the adversary and used to serve the needs of others for Christ and help free them from the chains of spiritual bondage. When God delivers you from sin, you will walk out free and victorious—with everything you need for the journey.

This was, no doubt, the reason for excitement and celebration for the Israelites: the sudden wealth and freedom after a lifetime of slavery. That last part was the real treasure. After so many years of slavery, not one of them had known what it was like to be free. All of this excitement flooded over them. Egypt and slavery grew distant in their rear-view mirror, with the Promised Land and freedom ahead.

Then comes chapter 13 and, along with it, a detour.

> When Pharaoh let the people go, God did not lead them
> by way of the land of the Philistines, although that was
> near. For God said, "Lest the people change their minds
> when they see war and return to Egypt." But God led the
> people around by the way of the wilderness toward the
> Red Sea. (Exodus 13:17, 18)

This was a huge detour! *Everyone* knew that the Philistine way along the coast was the quickest way to Canaan. It was between 150–200 miles, relatively easy terrain, and would get them there in only a few weeks. The desert road, on the other hand, was over 500 miles, had a rougher landscape, and would take quite a bit longer. Why the *desert* road? Why lead them so far out of the way? Wouldn't God want them in Canaan as soon as possible?

God told us why. They weren't ready. They weren't ready for Canaan and they weren't ready for the journey. The other way was too short to prepare them for what they would need to do to inhabit Canaan. As soon as they faced a major conflict (as we will learn, it wouldn't even need to be major), they would just turn and run back to slavery. You see, this is a common fact about mankind: we love to stay in our comfort zones. Oddly enough, Israel's comfort zone was slavery. That was what they knew and it was where they would run to should difficulty come their way. We are no different. Whether we will admit it or not, our "comfort zone" is sin. It is where we return when things get difficult. This is the human condition. So, in order to remove us from our area of comfort, we must be moved gradually.

Thus, Israel's detour had a purpose. God didn't send them the long way because there was unplanned construction on the Philistine road. He did it because He had a plan. There are three reasons this Divine Detour was part of God's plan.

First, God wanted to make them free. "Wait," you say. "They're leaving Egypt. Weren't they already free?" Sure, they were no longer obliged to do free labor for the Egyptians, but Egypt *still had their hearts and their minds*. Remember, they were in Egypt for over 400 years! However, they hadn't been slaves the whole time. They had originally come to Egypt as a blessing from God, as the people of God. After a few generations, the Pharaohs became afraid of their growing numbers and *gradually* made them slaves—like the "frog in the pot" lesson. Egypt slowly took away their freedom and slowly made them slaves of Egypt. Even worse, they slowly stripped Israel of their identity and made them think like Egyptians.

We know this plagued them throughout their journey because nearly every time they faced a difficult situation, they cried, "We wish we were back in Egypt!" You know, it's a sad day when you are on your way to freedom and all you can think of is how good it was back in slavery. It didn't matter if Israel groaned about how good Egypt was or how bad Egypt was; as long as Egypt was on their minds they weren't free from Egypt. So, since Egypt had gradually made them slaves (to the point that they would only think as slaves), God had to gradually free them. The detour was necessary because slaves are not always prepared for freedom. God knew it would take a process of reversal and renewal for them to become people who live and think like people who are free.

Many today would interject that they are slaves to no one, but this slave mindset still plagues humanity. If you are always worried about what someone else thinks about you, or if you think you must live up to someone else's standards—even a church's standard—you are thinking like a slave. As Paul wrote, "Do you not know that if you present yourselves to anyone as obedient slaves, you are slaves of the one whom you obey, either of sin, which leads to death, or of obedience, which leads to righteousness?" (Romans 6:16). Yes, we too are slaves. We are slaves, foremost, to sin, but we are also slaves of human expectations, religious traditions, societal norms, and our own passions.

But God wants us to be *completely* free. He desires us to be free from our fears, from our slave way of thinking, and from the chains of sin that keep our hearts and minds locked up. This kind of freedom takes time. If we want God to be King of our lives, we must be fully set free from everything and everyone else that tries to enslave us. Therefore, the extra time is worth it. And the promise in John 8:36 reminds us that "if the Son sets you free, you will be free indeed." If you are in Christ, you are no longer a slave to sin. So sometimes God takes us the long way around in order to fully remove slavery from within us and make us *completely* free.

It wasn't just freedom Israel needed, though. The detour was also necessary for God to make them strong. Remember, as they walked out of Egypt, they were recently unemployed slaves, not experienced gladiators. Most had no idea how to fight or, more likely, were afraid to. Egypt had crushed their spirits long before they left and Israel would easily back down if opposed. The best they could do was complain (one "talent" that stuck with them). Worse yet, not only did they not know how to fight, but they also didn't know *when* to fight, *who* to fight, or *why* to fight. Throughout their journey, they constantly fought the wrong people, at the wrong times, and for the wrong reasons. Israel was a disorganized, distrusting multitude. They would not be able to live in Canaan, with God as their King, if they remained that way.

God would have to change them to make them stronger—not physically stronger, though—He needed to make them a *unified, faith-filled army.* They had to learn to trust *God.* No future victories would be based on Israel's greatness, but on their willingness to follow Him. Because, when they arrived at the Promised Land, they would have to fight for it.* Don't miss this: to get to the place where God was the only Ruler in their lives, they would have to fight for it. They had to truly want it. Their former life of slavery would not give them up that easily. Yes, the land was promised, but there were still walls to overcome, giants to bring down, and kings to dethrone. A bunch of whiny, scaredy-cat, former slaves would be no match for what lay ahead.

Of course, a bunch of whiny, scaredy-cat, end-time Christians won't be a match for Satan's attacks today either. Jesus never said following Him would be easy. In fact, He said the opposite. He warned of great obstacles that laid ahead and giant deceptions

---

* This is another reason I believe the Promised Land represents our relationship with God more than it does Heaven. You do not have to fight for Heaven—it is already paid for. However, you will have to fight for God to be King of your life because there is a battle going on for the throne of your heart. And if you want God to reign on that throne, it will be a daily struggle.

that would attempt to defeat us (Matthew 24:24). He said that the world would hate us (John 15:18). Paul also reminds us that "we do not wrestle against flesh and blood" (Ephesians 6:12). In Revelation, John is shown that our Adversary would become tougher, and angrier: "But woe to you, O earth and sea, for the devil has come down to you in great wrath, because he knows that his time is short" (Revelation 12:12).

No, the journey to the Promised Land will not be easy. We will have to face some fortified obstacles, tear down giant fears, and dethrone idolatrous monarchs in our lives. We have no chance of survival if we turn and run at the first sign of opposition. We will not find success by complaining about our hardships and hiding in our comfort zones. God wants us to stand firm and trust *Him*. He wants us to know, and believe, that He is "our refuge and strength" (Psalms 46:1). It may take a detour in our life to make us truly learn to trust God. He may take us off our expected course so He can create in us faithful soldiers, fully trusting in His power.

This is vital because, ultimately, God led Israel on a detour in order to make them His again. Egypt had introduced many things to Israel, including strange ideas, morals, and other gods. While the Children of Israel were in slavery, they had grown accustomed to these new teachings. In fact, some had begun to believe in their authority and power. They had learned to love and to trust *Egypt*, and as long as they were not fully the Lord's, they would constantly run back into the arms of Egypt.

But God had made a covenant with them long before they were in Egypt, and He desired to renew it with them as they started their journey with Him. This had always been His desire: they would be *His children* and He would be *their God*. This would be the key to their success on the journey. It would be the key to their salvation. They would never be truly free or be truly strong if they didn't trust Him as *their* God. Thus, God gave them plenty of opportunities to see how He takes care of His people. They would soon learn that nothing could stand in their way as a nation under God; no one could oppose them when they were His people. So God took them on a detour because He wanted to give them time to learn to *run to Him*.

In a similar way, this world has introduced many ideas, morals, and gods to us as well and we have become accustomed to them—even to the point of falling in love with some of them. We have learned to put our trust in many things, and will run to them instead of to God. But God wants to make us His again. Throughout the ages He has called for us to come back to Him, so that He can be our God and we can be His people. It is even the foundation of God's last day message to mankind (Revelation 18:4).

This is what the journey is all about: He wants us to be *His* people. He wants us to run to Him when there's opposition. This doesn't happen overnight; it takes time. If it takes a detour, then so be it. Why? Because God wants to be *your* comfort and shield. He wants to be *your* financial advisor, *your* marriage counselor, *your* best friend, *your* father, *your* savior, and *your* God. He wants to be *yours* so you can be *His*.

We have learned to trust way too much in human wisdom. Right now, you may be faced with financial struggles—swamped with bills or facing too much month for your money—and you think the solution is some quick-fix advice from a financial guru. Friend, run to God. Maybe your marriage is going through a rough period and you're not sure it will last. You believe that if you could only attend a couples seminar or get advice from a counselor, everything will work out fine. Friend, run to God. It doesn't matter what your situation may be—run to God. While God may send help through other people, *He* is always the solution to your problem. This is why God wants to teach you to run to Him *first*. Understand that, on your journey with God, you will be continually faced with the same choice: run back to Egypt or run forward to God.

Why do we have detours? Why does God take us the long way sometimes? The answer is right here in the back seat: "The Lord is not slow to fulfill his promise as some count slowness, but is patient toward you, not wishing that any should perish, but that all should reach repentance" (2 Peter 3:9). God is not slow—He's not lost and wandering aimlessly—He is patient, so you can be completely free and full of faith. He's patient because He wants you. He wants you to trust Him, run to Him, and desire Him. Therefore, He'll take the long way around—if that is what it will take—so you can get to know Him.

Here is the truth: detours are simply part of our walk with God. The length of the detour, however, is up to you. It could be just a few weeks, or it could be forty years. The real pressing question is, how long will you have to walk on the detour before you'll trust Him enough to give yourself fully to Him?

"And Moses said to the people, 'Fear not, stand firm, and see the salvation of the LORD, which he will work for you today. For the Egyptians whom you see today, you shall never see again. The LORD will fight for you, and you have only to be silent.'"

EXODUS 14:13, 14

CHAPTER 2

FACING YOUR DEAD ENDS

The Israelites had only recently been freed from Egypt and were just starting their road trip. They were happy and free. Their instructions, so far, were simple: follow wherever God led. Fortunately for them, God made it easy for them to follow Him by leading them with a pillar of cloud by day and a pillar of fire by night (*way* better than GPS). All the Israelites had to do was follow that pillar.

However, not long after their exit from Egypt, God revealed a new plan to Moses (see Exodus 14:1–14). Even though they had already started traveling toward Canaan, God wanted them to turn back and go to a different campsite. It was a nice location on the Red Sea. You may have heard of it? It's the area in front of Pi-hahiroth, between Migdol and the sea. On second thought, maybe you haven't heard of it (you may not even be able to pronounce it). They weren't headed to this new location because it was known for its excellent camping facilities—it wasn't some luxurious beach destination—but rather, God chose this specific area to confuse Pharaoh. By choosing this place, God wanted Pharaoh to think that the Israelites were lost and locked in by the wilderness. This would prompt Pharaoh to decide to chase after them and bring them back. It may seem like a strange plan—they were just freed from Egypt. So why would God want Egypt to take them back? Well, He didn't. He wasn't planning on letting Pharaoh have them back. Instead, He was going to use this opportunity to teach Egypt who He really was—He is *the* LORD.

Of course, Israel didn't know about God's plan concerning Pharaoh—all they knew was that they had stopped on a beach at the Red Sea. To them, it may have been a nice oasis, especially after so many long, hard years making bricks as slaves. Can you picture the scene? Children entering the water and their parents yelling, "Don't wade past your armpits!" Beach balls and Frisbees (made in Egypt of course) filling the air. One Israelite family may have been barbecuing a little way down the beach. We do not read of one complaint voiced by the people when they first arrived. They were most likely enjoying their time at the Red Sea, with a beautiful view of the mountains all around.

Over in Egypt, the tune was different. Pharaoh and his men realized the impact on Egypt now that their main workforce was gone. Suddenly, their thoughts about Israel changed. One moment, they were glad to have them leave, but the next moment, they were asking, "What have we done?" Pharaoh noticed that Israel was trapped by the sea so he gathered all of his best chariots. Why stop there? He gathered all the other chariots, the not-as-good ones, and assembled his army. Then, with his great company of soldiers, he marched out to overtake this "god" of Israel and bring his slaves home.

Back on the beach, the joy and laughter suddenly stopped when somebody screamed. Everyone looked up to see what was happening. Terror filled their hearts when they saw Pharaoh and his army. Where was Moses when you needed him? All you would have had to do was follow the crowd. They were all headed to him to complain, as would become a habit for them, and there were experts in their midst.

You know who the "experts" are. Every group has at least one. They are the ones who love to point out the "reality" of a problem. They are the quickest to complain, yet the slowest to believe. They are "experts" in the ways of man, but ignorant in the ways of God.

Unfortunately, experts were among those in the crowd on our road trip with God's children. They squeezed their way to the front of the crowd because they had something to say. You have to read it to believe it:

> Is it because there are no graves in Egypt that you have taken us away to die in the wilderness? What have you done to us in bringing us out of Egypt? Is not this what we said to you in Egypt: "Leave us alone that we may serve the Egyptians"? For it would have been better for us to serve the Egyptians than to die in the wilderness. (Exodus 14:11, 12)

Wow. All of a sudden, they were angry with Moses for *saving them from slavery*. They saw this situation as worse than being someone else's slaves. The reality, as they saw it, loomed over them —mountains on either side, the Red Sea in front, and Pharaoh's army behind—there was no way out. They were at a dead end. The experts' opinion was offered: stop, give up, and go home. Quit the journey and go back to slavery.

Every now and then, we might find ourselves in a similar situation—especially on our journey with God. Trapped. Not by our surroundings, but by the views of "experts." Maybe you've heard their opinions of reality: *You'll never get out of debt. You'll never get well. You'll never amount to anything. You can't change. You're too young. You're too old.* Sometimes the "expert" is ourselves: *I can't do anything. I'm too sick. I'm not talented enough. I'm never going to change. I'm too young. I'm too old.*

Have you ever heard any of these? Have you ever said any of these? Maybe you feel like you have been painted into a dead end and think that there is no way out. I am sure every one of us has faced this. Unfortunately, far too often, when we are faced with an obstacle in our path, we listen to the "experts" and run back to our old way of life. But aren't you tired of being boxed in by "expert" opinions?

If so, I have good news for you. Dead ends are *not* stop signs. Think about it: when you come upon a Dead End sign on the road, you don't stop, turn off the car, and quit your trip, do you? No! You find an alternate way. So, when life's experts tell us that we're at a dead end, we need to look for a different solution—a second opinion—one that really matters: God's.

After the experts presented their opinion, God shared His view of Israel's reality: "Fear not, stand firm, and see the salvation of the LORD, which he will work for you today. For the Egyptians whom you see today, you shall never see again. The LORD will fight for you, and you have only to be silent" (Exodus 14:13, 14).

The experts' opinion was to go back to slavery. God's opinion was to continue forward to freedom. With the expert's solution, they would live with the Egyptians forever. With God's solution, they would never see those Egyptians again. Their answer was to stop, give up, and go home. But, God's instructions were to stop, give up, and go home.

You may be thinking, "Wait a minute, they're both saying the same thing!" Not really. They may be the same words, but they come from opposite perspectives—similar answers but very different outcomes. In order to see the difference, we need to look a little closer at God's instructions.

His first instruction is to *stop*. "Fear not," God says. In other words, stop your fears. Whenever we are faced with a progress-stopping obstacle, we must first stop being afraid. The reason this is so necessary is that fears alter our perspective. The Red Sea wasn't seen as a dead end at first. Israel's perspective changed once Pharaoh's army came into view. Fear didn't change their perspective on their surroundings or their pursuers—they knew the vastness of the sea and the strength of the Egyptian army— no, fear changed their perspective on *God*. The Red Sea and the Egyptians didn't grow, but in their minds, God shrank. Fear will always diminish our perception of God.

This is why we must stop our fears. They can distort our perspective of how great our God is! David reminds us in Psalms 27:1, "The LORD is my light and my salvation; whom shall I fear? The LORD is the stronghold of my life; of whom shall I be afraid?" Paul says in Romans 8:31, "If God is for us, who can be against us?" Yes, our God is *bigger* than any problem we can have. There is no problem He can't solve, no life He can't change, no sickness He can't cure, and no sinner He can't save. Our God is a big God. Our God is an *awesome* God! Therefore, we do not have to fear, because He is *our* God and our God is *with us*. So, God says, stop—do not be afraid.

Next, God instructs us to give up. That seems easy enough. The Israelites already had given up. They had their bags packed and were ready to go back to Egypt. But that was not what God meant. He wanted them to give *up*: "The LORD will fight for you, you have only to be silent" (Exodus 14:14). God wanted them to give up the battle, *not the journey*. This is also why they didn't need to be afraid: this wasn't their fight. God was going to fight for them, and all they had to do was to be still—to stop whining. Imagine if the Israelites had received the wish of their complaint or had tried to fight for themselves. They would've been back in Egypt and the book of Exodus would be 25 chapters shorter! The only way they would win the present, or any future, battle was to let God fight it.

Likewise, the spiritual battles in our lives aren't ours—they never have been ours—they are God's. Every time we are attacked, He is attacked. Every time we advance, He advances. Yet, we persistently try to fight our battles by ourselves—as if we are some kind of spiritual Rambos. We should know what happens to us if we give up or take on the enemy alone. We lose! We only end up back where we started. But if that was where we really wanted to be, why start following God in the first place? No, we leave our old lives because of the new life God promises. Why would we settle for less? God doesn't want us to go back either. He wants to rescue us from our past—our slavery to sin—and bring us to the Promised Land. This is why God fights for us: because *He will win*. He always does (there's plenty of evidence in the Bible of His amazing success rate).

Once we stop and give *up*, He tells us to *go home*. This is where the Israelites were most often confused. This is where we still get confused. Why? Because, is home where you've been, or where you're going? Notice what God said: "Why do you cry to me? Tell the people of Israel to go *forward*" (Exodus 14:15, emphasis mine). You're not home yet. Keep moving *forward*; stay on course. Home is on the *other* side. They couldn't just sit there and sulk. God told them to keep moving.

This can be the hardest thing to do when we are facing great obstacles. In front of us may be a sea of reasons to sit still or turn around. Behind us might stand the army of our enemy designed to intimidate us into forfeiting. When we focus on those obstacles, we often become afraid to take steps of faith and follow God. Yet the Bible encourages us to "walk in all the way that the LORD your God has commanded you, that you may live and that it may go well with you" (Deuteronomy 5:33).

But, what does it mean that "it may go well with you"? Will we all become millionaires and have big houses and nice cars? Although people may wish that is what this phrase means, it isn't.

We learn what it means by examining what happened when the Israelites followed God's instructions. Remember the rest of the story (Exodus 14:16–22)? God told Moses to raise his staff over the sea, which would divide the sea, and then the Israelites could cross. Not only did they cross the sea, but they also crossed it on dry ground. I want to make sure you understand how amazing this was. It was previously a *sea*, but it became *dry ground*—with walls of water on both sides! It wasn't muddy, sloppy ground—it was completely dry. They didn't even get their feet wet! The lesson here: *we will not experience the amazing things God wants to do in our lives, unless we move forward.* He can do far more than we can ask for—and He usually does. But we have to be willing to move. He'll take care of the rest. And believe me, He will.

We know this because God is faithful. God said that they would never see those Egyptians again—and they didn't. It is amazing to me that Pharaoh and his army actually chased the Israelites out onto the dry seabed. I can't imagine being a soldier in that army, seeing the walls of water mysteriously parted on either side, and thinking, "I want to go in there!" They must have been filled with incredible rage toward the Israelites. Rage will do that to a person. It can make a person do very stupid things (like race out onto a recently, and miraculously, dried seabed with walls of water on either side). So they chased the Israelites onto the dry seabed, but God threw them into confusion and made it difficult to drive their chariots. It became so bad that the soldiers came to their senses and tried to convince Pharaoh to retreat—even the soldiers realized that Israel's God was fighting against them. As they fled, God instructed Moses to stretch his staff across the sea and the sea went back to its place, washing away the army of Pharaoh. According to Exodus 14:28, *not one* Egyptian survived.*

---

* Some argue that the place where the Israelites crossed wasn't very deep, maybe only a few inches of water. Even if this was the case, it is still a huge miracle—a greater one even—because that would mean God drowned the whole Egyptian army in ankle-deep water!

When God tells you that He will take care of you, He will. God will not lead you to a place where He cannot deliver you.

Still, every one of us will be faced with a Red Sea to cross—a seemingly dead end. You may find yourself trapped in a corner surrounded by mountains of troubles and a sea of doubt, with your past life pursuing to enslave you again. And, no doubt, "experts" will be present, pointing out your problems while giving you free advice.

Their advice is always the same. They will tell you to stop— you're at a dead end. So, stop the car, turn off the ignition, and end your trip. You might as well give up—give up on your goals and your God because your problems are too big for either of you anyway. Why did you even start this journey? You should just go home—go back to where you came from. You have gone as far as you can. You were never going to make it all the way anyway. Good try, but now you're at a dead end, so turn around and go back to Egypt. Back to slavery: this is the only place human wisdom can take you.

But God says, "Stop. Stop your fears. You don't have to be afraid. Know that I am bigger than any of your problems. I am stronger than all of your enemies. I am your Shield. I am your Strength. I am your Savior. Do not be afraid because I Am *your* God and I will never leave you. Since I am right here with you, give *up*. Give your burdens and your battles to me. Let me fight for you. Let me win for you. And keep going home. No, you are not home yet—so keep moving forward. Go to your Red Sea and go *through* your Red Sea. *Your home is on the other side, so you have to keep moving*." All the way Home: this is where God will take you.

Is this not why you started your journey with God in the first place? To go home to the land of promise where there is no more sickness, suffering, or death? Then why turn back? Why give up? There are no obstacles on your journey too big to overcome, because those are God's battles, not yours.

If you have found yourself at a dead end, please don't quit your journey. Don't give up on God. Don't forfeit and return to slavery. Instead, let the promise of the presence of God calm your fears. Trust Him. Stand firm and let Him fight for you. Keep walking. Follow Him all the way home.

"And he said to me, 'It is done! I am the Alpha and the Omega, the beginning and the end. To the thirsty I will give from the spring of the water of life without payment. The one who conquers will have this heritage, and I will be his God and he will be my son.'"

REVELATION 21:6, 7

CHAPTER 3

NEVER THIRST AGAIN

Deeply involved in a massive game of UNO (we had combined three decks) in the back seat of the van, I was blissfully unaware of the trouble about to occur. Loud, angry, screeching sounds abruptly spilled out from the front, and the van began to lurch and sputter. The dashboard became alive with color. As quickly as the convulsions of the engine had begun, they stopped—and so did the van. As we drifted to the side of the road, our hearts sank.

It was 1985 and I was with a group of kids on our way to Camp Hale, Colorado for the first International Pathfinder* Camporee. It was a big deal. Boys and girls from all over the world were going to be there. Our Pathfinder group had raised and saved all the money needed for the trip. We had rented two vans, packed them with all of our necessities, and embarked on a journey

---

*Pathfinders is a group within the Seventh-day Adventist Church organization for boys and girls, ages ten to fifteen years, that focuses on their cultural, social, and religious education. While it is similar to Boy and Girl Scouts, it differs by the religious emphasis on their activities.

from Michigan to the great Rocky Mountains. Nevertheless, at that moment, about a dozen of us children were sitting in our van *broken down* on the side of the road.

Our leader stepped out of the van and lifted the hood, billows of white smoke pouring out. It didn't take long to find the problem: due to the strong sun and heavy climbing, the engine had overheated. To make matters worse, in spite of our precautions and the unabridged list of things to bring, we had forgotten a very important item: extra water. We had taken it for granted and were now paying for it.

Endless time seemed to pass as we waited outside the van for the engine to cool down. With the sun overhead, it wasn't long before we too began to overheat. Thirst began to take control. Our tongues dried up and our lips cracked. Dizziness and weakness settled in. Consciousness drifted in and out. Vultures began to circle overhead. Our frail little bodies lay there, drying up on the side of the road. Weeks later, they would find only our bones, next to an overheated rental van. At least, that's what my eleven-year-old imagination had concluded.

I did not know which was worse, not having water for the van, or not having water for me. It's interesting how you can become very thirsty the moment you realize there isn't any water to drink. Just then, someone spotted a stream down a hill on the other side of the road. In no time, we had our radiator filled, as well as our water bottles, and we were on our way. We were fortunate, but such a breakdown—running dry—has ended many journeys early.

Of course, no one will argue the importance of water. You can go without food much longer than you can go without water. It is vital for life. Yet, sadly, it is often taken for granted, leaving many thirsty. It is said that by the time you feel thirst you are already dehydrated.

On our trip with the Children of Israel we find ourselves thirsty as well. Three times as a matter of fact. Three times, our

Promised Land charter bus overheats. As we sit on the side of the road next to the overheated bus, we learn a few lessons about ourselves and about God.

The first incident is recorded in Exodus 15. The Israelites had only recently left the Red Sea and walked for three days without finding any water. Arriving at Marah, they finally found some . . . kind of. "When they came to Marah, they could not drink the water of Marah because it was bitter" (Exodus 15:23). You can imagine that after three days of walking in the desert, the sight of water would be very inviting. But the water was "bitter." Scholars cannot completely agree about what is meant by it being bitter. Some say it had unhealthy bacteria while others believe it was salty, but one thing is for sure: they couldn't drink it. This is almost worse than not having water at all!

God reveals the cause of bitter water on our journey: "My people have committed two sins: They have forsaken me, the spring of living water, and have dug their own cisterns, broken cisterns that cannot hold water" (Jeremiah 2:13 NIV). They had forgotten about God. They were not going to God with their spiritual thirst, but were trying to quench it using their own methods. They were trying to survive on their journey with God *without God*. The result: "Consider then and realize how *evil and bitter it is for you when you forsake the* LORD *your God and have no awe of me*" (Jeremiah 2:19 NIV, emphasis mine). When we forget about or abandon God, our lives become bitter. When we try to do things *our* way—try to fill the God-shaped void with the things we *do*—we are left thirsty and bitter. Indeed, bitterness invades our lives when we lose our awe of God.

Already forgetting about God, Israel reverted to their natural talent (it's not a spiritual gift, by the way): grumbling to Moses. Sadly, bitterness often turns into whining. They had forgotten about the miracle of the Red Sea after only three days! They could only see what was in front of them: bitter water. It is sad how quickly we can forget recent demonstrations of the power of God. We all have bad days, bad weeks, or even a bad year. Yet, why is it that, when we go through a spiritual trial that ends with undrinkable water, we completely forget all of the blessings God has given to us up to that point? Nevertheless, while Israel's story warns us of this danger on our journey, it also reminds us that there is a solution.

Moses did what they should have done: he went to God. God showed Moses a piece of wood—a tree—and instructed him to throw it into the water. Moses obeyed and the water became sweet (fresh). In other words, they could drink it! Our lesson from this is that only God can take the bitterness out of our lives. He says, "If you will diligently listen to the voice of the LORD your God, and do that which is right in his eyes, and give ear to his commandments and keep all his statutes, I will put none of the diseases on you that I put on the Egyptians, for I am the LORD, your healer" (Exodus 15:26). God says, *listen to me—trust me and follow me— and then I can heal you.* I will make your bitter water sweet. No matter how bad the situation may be, He can turn it around.

All they had to do was throw a piece of wood in the water. Have you ever wondered why God had Moses toss a chunk of wood into the water? It wasn't just a random idea. God does not do things without a purpose. There was a reason it was a piece of wood. Consider the cross: not too long ago, our Savior hung on a tree that can turn our bitter into sweet. The cross reminds us of God's power and love. In the shadow of the cross, your journey *cannot* remain bitter! Maybe life is beginning to feel bitter because it has been too long since you've sat at the foot of the cross. If the bitterness on our journey is because we have abandoned God, then the solution is to return to Him. Add the cross to your "bitter pond" (by spending time reading about Jesus' sacrifice for your life and meditating on it—beholding your Savior) and watch the water become sweet!

However, sometimes there isn't any water at all. Not even bitter water. We join God's children on the side of the road for the second time in Exodus 17. This was the first time in Israel's journey that they were totally without water. And, once again, they grumbled to extremes: "Why did you bring us up out of Egypt, to kill us and our children and our livestock with thirst?" (Exodus 17:3). This time, they brought their kids and animals into it. Again, Moses turned to God and learned what he was to do next (Exodus 17:5, 6).

Once again, God's instructions were simple. This time, Moses was to go to a rock, where God would be standing, and strike it with his staff. The instructions were simple, but not very typical. One doesn't learn in a wilderness survival class to strike a rock in order to get water. This isn't how nature usually works. Can you imagine how this plan sounded to Moses? Nevertheless, Moses obeyed and water *gushed* out of the rock—enough for the whole camp, including their children and livestock.

Although the miracle itself was awesome enough, there was also an important message within it. A message that Paul explains in his first letter to the Corinthians: "[They] all drank the same spiritual drink. For they drank from the spiritual Rock that followed them, and the Rock was Christ" (1 Corinthians 10:4). God used the rock as a symbol of His Son. Jesus was the Spiritual Rock that accompanied them and gave them the water for life. As a result of the presence of the Rock, "They did not thirst when he led them through the deserts; he made water flow for them from the rock" (Isaiah 48:21). It is kind of hard to believe, yet, they didn't thirst the *whole time* they were in *the desert*. God is amazing.

What this means is that when Jesus accompanies you on the journey, you will never be without the Living Water. Just as the rock of Exodus 17 was struck, unleashing a fountain of water, so also was our Rock (Jesus) struck, flooding us with a fountain of *life* (see John 7:38 and 19:34). We don't have to thirst in this barren wilderness called Earth. We have a Rock—we have *the* Rock—the Source of life-giving water: Jesus. Once again, the solution to quenching our spiritual thirst is Jesus.

In spite of a lack of faith the first time they were at the border of the Promised Land (we'll talk more about this in chapters 9 and 10), God kept His promise, and we do not hear of a water shortage throughout their wanderings in the desert. Israel's needs were supplied for *forty years.* They had become content with God's blessings of water until they were almost in Canaan. It is at this point in their journey that we find our third story.

According to the story (Numbers 20:1–6), forty years later—on the edges of the land of Canaan—Israel found themselves thirsty again on the edge of the road. Now, a new generation of Israelites began to whine. Even worse, the Bible says they gathered themselves together *against* Moses and Aaron. They did not go to Moses simply to complain, they went to attack.[†] Amazingly, in their grumbling, they actually said it would have been better if they had died with their parents in the wilderness! It is hard to imagine how people can become so ungrateful.

Once again, Moses went to God and, once again, God told Moses to go to the rock. The instructions seemed similar but, this time, there was a twist: God told Moses to "Take the staff, and assemble the congregation, you and Aaron your brother, and tell the rock before their eyes to yield its water. So you shall bring water out of the rock for them and give drink to the congregation and their cattle" (Numbers 20:7, 8).

Earlier, God told Moses to *strike* the rock, but this time He told Him to only *speak* to it. Sadly, Moses struck the rock anyway

---

[†] This, by the way, is not a very productive way to deal with a difficult situation. Attacking and blaming everything on our leaders will not benefit us. Bad things happen even with the best leaders. Regardless of who the leader is, we should want them to succeed in leading us well. Instead of meeting to tear them down, we should meet to lift them up. Especially when things aren't going well, we need to lift our leaders in prayer.

(verse 11). Maybe he struck it out of frustration. The people had just verbally attacked him. Maybe he struck it out of habit. We are not told how many times during their desert journey Moses may have struck a rock to get water. Regardless of the reason why he struck the rock, we know that he did—and not just once, but twice! He disobeyed God's direct command and dishonored Him. (This is evidence that even great leaders of God still fail sometimes. It is a strong reminder that we all can, and do, fall short of God's glory.)

Still, why the difference? Why did God instruct Moses to only speak to the rock this time? We saw earlier that Jesus was struck, like the rock, to pour out the spring of living water. This symbolized the crucifixion. However, we know that three days later, He rose from the grave—never to die again, never to be *struck* again. Also, in John 4:10, when Jesus was talking to the Samaritan woman, He said: "If you knew the gift of God, and who it is that is saying to you, 'Give me a drink,' you would have *asked* him, and he would have given you living water" (emphasis mine). All we need to do now is ask. It is the natural progression of learning to depend fully on Him. We rely less on our own actions (striking the rock), and instead, learn to rely more on His love and mercy by simply asking. When we do, He will give us the water described in verse 14: "whoever drinks of the water that I will give him will never be thirsty again. The water that I will give him will become in him a spring of water welling up to eternal life." When we receive the water Christ gives, it becomes a well inside us, never running dry. We won't thirst again because the fountain is *within* us. There's no catch: Jesus says, if you are thirsty, come. This is God's message for us today: you don't have to thirst ever again.

Of course, with all this talking about water and deserts you might be getting thirsty yourself. Is this what Jesus was talking about: never thirsting for physical water? What is it for which we thirst? David gives us a clue: "As the deer pants for streams of water, so my soul pants for you, my God" (Psalm 42:1 NIV). Have you ever seen a deer panting for water? I haven't. I would imagine that it would take an extreme thirst for them to pant. Likewise, the thirst Jesus is talking about is an extreme desire for God; it is a deep desire to know Him.

Perhaps you have become more thirsty lately for a deeper relationship with God. On our journey from slavery in sin to the Promised Land where God is our King, our relationship with Him must grow. This is where the thirsting comes in. When this spiritual thirst enters our lives it is a sign that we are becoming God-dehydrated. The only solution is to saturate ourselves again with His presence.

Maybe all you have experienced in your journey with God is bitterness. It doesn't matter what has made your journey bitter, the solution is always the same: go to the cross. The cross reminds us of God's love and how much He wants to have a relationship with us. Spend some time reading and contemplating Jesus' last moments before the cross. Experience the cross again. Throw it in the midst of the bitterness, and then watch. Watch as Jesus' hands and feet are nailed into the wood. Watch as He forgives you. Watch as He dies for *your* sins. *Watch*. Because you will not come away from the cross bitter. The cross changes the relationship. It changes the bitter into sweet.

When you are at the cross, you are looking at the source of living water, the Rock of our Salvation. Jesus was bruised, spit on, laughed at, kicked, mocked, and struck so your relationship with Him could begin to really flow. He was crucified so you could have the opportunity to drink from this River of Life, and He rose again, never to be struck again, so that while you journey in this barren wasteland of a Godless society, you don't have to thirst for a relationship with Him. All you have to do is ask. Just *speak* to the Rock and the Water of Life will pour out. If you are willing to ask, you could be filled with this never-ending spring of living water.

This is why, in the last book of the Bible, Jesus sends out this invitation: "It is done! I am the Alpha and the Omega, the beginning and the end. To the thirsty I will give from the spring of the water of life without payment [*it's free!*]. The one who conquers will have this heritage, and I will be his God and he will be my son" (Revelation 21:6, 7, note mine).

This is what Jesus died for: to make our relationship with Him permanent—to make it eternal. But you don't have to wait until Heaven to quench your thirst for a relationship with God. You can have a relationship with Him here and now! Yes! The God of the universe *wants* to have a relationship with you. If you are thirsty—thirsty to know God—come to Him and drink. Be filled with the Water of Life that flows from the throne of God. Come, let Him keep you from ever thirsting for Him again. All of heaven is waiting. Waiting to fill your cup, fill your soul. Waiting for you to ask. How thirsty are you though? Are you "panting as a deer" thirsty? Praise God, you never have to thirst again. Just kneel before God right now and ask to be filled with this living water.

"Now therefore, if you will indeed obey my voice and keep my covenant, you shall be my treasured possession among all peoples, for all the earth is mine; and you shall be to me a kingdom of priests and a holy nation."

Exodus 19:5, 6

CHAPTER 4

THE IMPORTANCE OF FOLLOWING INSTRUCTIONS

As I walked into the classroom I was confident. It may have been because I had learned a secret about our teacher: his tests were easy. I believed this because I was told that his tests were mostly multiple choice, and I was good at multiple choice. When the time for his first test came, I was ready.

After my teacher handed me the test, I glanced down at it. My "insider information" was right: it was packed with multiple choice questions. There *was* an essay at the end, but I had learned how to handle them as well. This test would be a breeze. I put my name on the top and began. I was several questions into the test when the teacher interrupted my progress. "Make sure you read the instructions and follow them carefully," he said to the class.

Ah, teacher naivety. I knew they had to say that stuff for those who didn't know, but I knew. I mean, I had read those kind of instructions before—many times. I knew them well enough that I didn't need to read *these* specifically. *Everyone knows how to do multiple choice*, I thought.

It wasn't long before I finished the multiple choice questions and turned to the essay. There was one question at the top, and the rest of the page was blank. I knew the basic idea of what he was asking—I could have answered it in a couple of sentences, but that wouldn't fill the whole page. I knew I needed to fill the page, but I wasn't worried because I also knew what every teacher wanted when they gave an essay question: words—big words— and lots of them. Everyone knows that the more words you use the more educated you sound. The larger your vocabulary, the more scholarly you appear. The more copious your vernacular, the greater your enlightenment is perceived to be, even if you're just repeating the same thing over and over. So, I dug deep into my vast, collegiate vocabulary and began to write. In no time, my "Shakespearean" masterpiece was done. I waited for a couple minutes, of course—I didn't want it to look like the test was too easy. After a couple of my classmates had turned in their tests, I proudly walked up to the front of the class and handed mine to the teacher.

A few days later, the test results came back and the teacher handed our tests back to us. I could feel the excitement building. When I finally received my test, I quickly turned it over to see my grade. And then it fell—my excitement as well as the test. *I had failed.* How? I had known all the answers. There had to be a mistake! I promptly brought my test to the teacher and asked him why my grade was so low. Without even looking up, he asked, "Did you follow the instructions?"

I was a bit offended—they were multiple choice questions, how hard could they be? "Of course!" I said, pointing to the test. "Choose the correct answer: A, B, C, or . . ." *Oh no.* The directions said to choose *all* of the correct answers. I found out that each question had *more than one* correct answer. Sure enough, although I may have had one right, I missed the others—many others. I quickly turned to my essay: out of twenty points I only received five. As I opened my mouth with my next objection, he pointed again to the test. The instructions said to write the answer *in two or three sentences*. No more. No less. The teacher wasn't interested in my novella; he only wanted the simple idea.

How important is it to follow instructions? I can tell you firsthand that it can be the deciding factor in whether you pass or fail. Now, I'm sure I am not the only one who has ever underestimated the importance of following instructions. Maybe you are the type of person who will only pull out the instructions if there are pieces left over. Or, maybe you have said this before: "I don't *need* directions. I'm not lost, I just don't recognize where I am at the moment."

I need to make something clear though. This is not about the importance of following just any instructions, but about following the instructions of the One who is leading. My error in the class was that I had followed the instructions of another teacher, or one of my friends, not the instructions of the teacher who was giving me the test. Likewise, I may be following the instructions of a pastor, or a church, but I need to be following the instructions of God. "They are the same thing," you may say. Not necessarily. Both the Bible and history show us that mankind has, at times, come up with commands that God never gave. Every instruction on our spiritual journey needs to come directly from, or be verified by, God and His Word. If God is leading, His instructions are the ones that are important to follow.

Even then, we still may ask, is it really necessary to follow *every* instruction? If you've heard one, haven't you heard them all? Of course, we'll hear the same question from the back seat on our journey to the Promised Land.

They had made some progress down the road—all the way to Exodus 16. Unfortunately, they found themselves in a situation that seemed to require some well-practiced whining:

And the people of Israel said to [Moses and Aaron], "Would that we had died by the hand of the LORD in the land of Egypt, when we sat by the meat pots and ate bread to the full, for you have brought us out into this wilderness to kill this whole assembly with hunger." (Exodus 16:3)

Ladies and gentlemen, these aren't the Children of Israel—they are the Teenagers of Israel. Such drama! "There's nothing to eat! I'm going to die of hunger!" (Unfortunately this behavior only gets worse along this trip.) I've never understood how they went so quickly to such extremes in their whining. For some reason, every obstacle resulted in dying. On this occasion, they grumbled that it would have been better to die in Egypt rather than to die in the desert. Either way, they would still be *dead*. Furthermore, if they had recalled their recent thirsting dilemma, they would have remembered that God would take care of them. He had brought water *from a rock*. What would be next, pizza from a tree? It wouldn't be impossible for God to feed them. Still, when their stomachs started grumbling, so did their mouths: "Are you trying to starve us to death?" What they did not know was that God already had the solution, but it came with a set of instructions.

Behold, I am about to rain bread from heaven for you, and the people shall go out and gather a day's portion every day, that I may test them, whether they will walk in my law or not. On the sixth day, when they prepare what they bring in, it will be twice as much as they gather daily. (Exodus 16:4, 5)

It sounded easy enough. They were to go out every morning and gather this "bread from Heaven," and then on the sixth day gather twice as much. That couldn't be too hard, could it? You wouldn't think so. But, did you catch the reason God gave for the instructions? To *test* them and see if they would fully follow Him. Sometimes we think that God is burdening us with little, insignificant instructions, even though it is the little things that prove to God that we are truly willing to follow Him.

Remember, this is what the journey is all about: learning to completely depend on God. So, sometimes God will put something in your life—tests, if you will—to see if you will trust Him and obey. All the Children of Israel had to do was listen to, and follow, God's instructions. Everyone heard the instructions, but were they all listening? Would they pass the test?

Just as God had said, there was quail in the evening and some white stuff on the ground in the morning (Exodus 16:13–15). They recognized the quail, but this stuff in the morning confused them. They had never seen it before. This should clue us in on something pretty significant: God's promises do not always come in a way we will recognize. Just because we do not get exactly what we expect does not mean it is not a blessing from God. Israel surely didn't recognize their "blessing" from God—they called it *manna*, which means, "What is it?" This makes me think of the similarly named candy bar, *Whatchamacallit*, or even the "mystery loaf" (an end-of-the-week dish often made from leftovers and other undisclosed ingredients) served at the cafeteria when I was in college. The Israelites had no idea what the white stuff was, but it was good. (Of course it was good—it came from heaven!)

Moses explained that this strange white stuff on the ground was the bread from heaven that God promised. He then re-explained God's instructions. Basically, everyone was supposed to gather only enough for their family: one omer (about two quarts) for each person in their tent. Everyone gathered what they needed and, amazingly, they all had enough for that day. So far, so good. Moses also reminded them not to keep any until the next morning or it would spoil (verse 19). We may be quick to wonder, why? Remember, this was a test to see if they would trust Him and obey.

How quickly we find some who didn't listen. God said that He would provide for them *every* day. The instructions were simple: use everything He's given today, and tomorrow He'll send more. However, some must not have trusted what Moses said. Maybe they didn't believe that the instructions were worth following. They trusted their own instincts instead. What they did next was not about saving for the future, it was about a lack of trust in God. They were not being frugal; rather, they were being faithless. Their lack of trust resulted in rotten manna—God's blessing spoiled (verse 20).

This morning blessing went on, and the story continues. Every day, for six days, they gathered what they needed for the day. Then, God explained the next part of the instructions: the rules that governed the days of the week did not apply on the seventh day. On the Sabbath, no manna would fall—it was to be a day of rest for the people. So, instead of gathering it on Sabbath morning, they were to gather *twice* as much the day before. All the extra manna gathered on the sixth day would stay fresh to be used on Sabbath (verses 23–26).

You can imagine that the people who saved the manna days before were a little hesitant about saving it this time. Sure enough, verse 27 says that some still went out on Sabbath to gather manna. They may not have been the same people as before, but once again, the lack of listening abounded. God told them that the leftover manna would last because there was something special about the seventh day. He wanted the seventh day to be a holy day for them, as it was at creation (Genesis 2:1–3). However, it is obvious that some didn't believe the manna would stay fresh. The passage says that they went looking for food, but they didn't find any. Not one flake. I'd bet the next week they saved some.

That Sabbath morning, the first tests were handed back. So how did they do? Did they pass? "How long will you refuse to keep my commandments and my laws? See! The LORD has given you the Sabbath; therefore on the sixth day he gives you bread for two days. Remain each of you in his place; let no one go out of his place on the seventh day" (Exodus 16:28, 29). Uh oh. Many of them failed. "How long will it take until you trust Me?" He asked. "I did this for *you*. I *gave* you the Sabbath! How long will you fight my instructions. When will you just follow me?"

This is what His instructions were about. They seemed like trivial rules. Did it really matter how much they gathered or if they saved it? No. God was not rationing the manna—it was not as if God only had it in limited supply. It was not about the Sabbath day either. It was about trusting Him enough to follow *any* command He might give—no matter how unusual it sounded (like walking around a city to take down its walls). He wanted the Israelites, and us, to know that *great things come from following His instructions*, even the simple ones. His instructions are not meant to burden us, but to free us—to bless us. Having the Sabbath off was a gift that came as a result of following what God said, but God had something greater in mind.

God's purpose wasn't to teach Israel how to correctly gather food during the week; He wanted them to be His "treasured possession" among the nations—to become a kingdom of priests and a holy nation (Exodus 19:5, 6). Have you ever thought of yourself as God's treasured possession? Yet, becoming fully and truly His is where following His instructions will lead. Through these experiences, He wants to teach us that if we will follow His commands, He will be able to *bless us in ways we can't begin to imagine*. If a fully free day of rest (the Sabbath) was the gift from desert instructions on manna gathering, how much greater are the things He will give from His Eternal instructions?

Of course, there is an opposite to all of this. If we fail to listen and obey, there are consequences. Though God will forgive us for disobedience and rebellion against Him when we repent (1 John 1:9), we still have to live with the consequences of our choices.

Sadly, disobedience and rebellion are often what the Israelites chose. They didn't always see the importance of following His instructions. As a result, they didn't become the Holy nation or the kingdom of priests. Instead, they were enslaved by pagan nations over and over. Unfortunately, they frequently failed the test.

How important do you think it is to follow instructions? Solomon said in Ecclesiastes 12:13, "The end of the matter; all has been heard. Fear God and keep his commandments, for this is the whole duty of man." Solomon learned through his experiences in life that fearing God and following His commands was all that really mattered—it was the whole duty of man. Everything else was worthless.

Nevertheless, some today argue that keeping God's commands is no longer necessary. They consider any modern attempt to keep God's laws as legalistic—trying to earn a way into heaven through works. They suggest that God's instructions have been thrown out—that Jesus got rid of them (at least ten of the big ones) —and we are now only under grace. If this is so, then why did Jesus tells us in John 14:15, "If you love me, you will keep my commandments"? According to Jesus, if we love Him, we *will* obey Him. Anyone in a relationship with Him will follow all of His instructions. Obedience to God's commands is not about salvation by works. Obedience is about establishing a dependent relationship with Him. Of course, if we confess to be followers of Christ, and if we desire a relationship with Him, how can we not listen and obey? But He's talking about new commands, not those old ones right?

Jesus summed up all of His instructions once, as simply as possible: "You shall love the Lord your God with all your heart and with all your soul and with all your mind. This is the great and first commandment. And a second is like it: You shall love your neighbor as yourself. On these two commandments depend all the Law and the Prophets" (Matthew 22:37–40). This is what *all* of the Law and the Prophets are about. Every word from God to man is founded on these two principles. This is what we will obey if we love Jesus.

You see, His instructions are not meant to burden you, but to set you free; they will lead you to greater things. If you love the Lord your God with all that you are, you will find yourself doing all that you can to build and strengthen your relationship with Him and reflect more of His character in your life. When you love God as you should, you become a part of a holy people, a holy church. And if you love your neighbors as Jesus loved you (John 13:34), you will find yourself loving unconditionally and sharing the message of salvation with more love and grace. When you love another person with Christ-like love, you become a part of a priestly people, a priestly church. This is the result of following God's instructions: a holy, priestly people treasured by God.

God's desire on this journey is to teach you to depend on Him—to trust that He will bring you to greater things, both individually and as a group (church). So, how important is it to follow instructions? It makes all the difference in the world.

"And I will establish my covenant between me and you and your offspring after you throughout their generations for an everlasting covenant, to be God to you and to your offspring after you."

GENESIS 17:7

CHAPTER 5

MAKiNG IT OFFICiAL

About three months after Israel left Egypt, they entered into the wilderness of Sinai and set up camp. Some may only connect the mountain in this area with Israel receiving a couple of tablets of laws, but something much greater took place at the foot of the mountain. For three months, they had experienced the leading, instruction, and care of God. They watched as God gave them freedom from the Egyptians at the Red Sea. They saw with their own eyes water pouring from a rock and food coming from heaven. They had even witnessed miraculous military victories with God's leading (Exodus 17:8–13). It was with all of this evidence of His care and protection that God brought them to Mount Sinai for the next step: making their blossoming relationship official.

As we have learned, this whole journey was about God freeing His people from Egypt. He wasn't just transporting them to a new location; His goal was to get them back as *His*. Now, at the base of the Mountain of Sinai, God was going to pop the question.

He desired to tie the knot. No, even more than that: He was prepared to enter into a covenant with them. He wanted to know if they were ready to be completely His.

Much like today, a covenant in the days of Israel was an agreement between people. In most cases, two individuals were involved, with each party having some requirements to hold up their end of the contract. Once a covenant had been entered into, it lasted as long as was stated in the conditions—unless it was broken (as they often were). But breaking the covenantal terms came with consequences.

Of the many covenants of the Bible, most had no impact on anyone else but the individuals mentioned in it. There were covenants between two humans, like the one between Laban and Jacob (Genesis 31:44). While their covenant was made based on a lack of trust, there were some made between best friends as well, like the one between Jonathan and David (1 Samuel 18:3). There are also examples of when God entered into a covenant with an individual. God made a covenant with Noah vowing to deliver him and his family from the flood (Genesis 6:18). He made a covenant with Abraham confirming His promise to make him a father of many nations (Genesis 17:2, 4). He also made a covenant with Phinehas promising a permanent priesthood (Numbers 25:12, 13).

Finally, there are covenants made between God and a group of people (mainly the Israelites*). Of these, only two covenants impacted all of mankind, one of which was promising to not destroy mankind again with a flood (Genesis 9:9–17). The other covenant God made with all of mankind is often missed—partly because it appears to be made with an individual, Abraham. However, it also concerned his offspring (some translations say "seed"). It may be easy to assume that Abraham's offspring simply

---

* For examples of covenants God made specifically with Israel, see Exodus 31:16 and Exodus 34:10.

refers to the Israelites, but we must keep in mind what Paul wrote: "And if you are Christ's then you are Abraham's offspring, heirs according to the promise" (Galatians 3:29). Abraham's offspring represents all who follow God as Abraham did—in faith. This covenant was not made with a specific nation or a specific bloodline in mind, but with all who chose to walk with God.

The foundation of this covenant is first mentioned in Genesis 17:7, where God told Abraham, "And I will establish my covenant between me and you and your offspring after you throughout their generations for an everlasting covenant, to be God to you and to your offspring after you." In this covenant God says, "I will be your God." It is not a covenant of boundaries or duties; it is a covenant of *relationship*. And this covenantal-relationship language continues throughout the Bible:

> ... that *you may enter into the sworn covenant* of the LORD your God, which the LORD your God is making with you today, *that He may establish you today as His people, and that He may be your God,* as He promised you, and as He swore to your fathers, to Abraham, to Isaac, and to Jacob. (Deuteronomy 29:12, 13, emphasis mine)

> I will give them a heart to know that I am the LORD, and *they shall be my people and I will be their God,* for they shall return to me with their whole heart. (Jeremiah 24:7, emphasis mine)

> I will save them from all the backslidings in which they have sinned, and will cleanse them; and *they shall be my people, and I will be their God. . . . I will make a covenant of peace with them* . . . My dwelling place shall be with them, and *I will be their God, and they shall be my people.* (Ezekiel 37:23, 26, 27, emphasis mine)

. . . and they shall be my people, and I will be their God, in faithfulness and in righteousness. (Zechariah 8:8, emphasis mine)

God is clear about His intent with this covenant: He wants to be our God and He wants us to be His people. Again, lest we assume that this covenant was only for Israel, this is what John wrote in the second to last chapter of Revelation: "And I heard a loud voice from the throne saying, 'Behold the dwelling place of God is with man. He will dwell with them, and *they will be his people, and God himself will be with them as their God'*" (Revelation 21:3, emphasis mine). When all is said and done—when sin is no more and the earth is made new—this is the relationship God will have with *all* of His people. It is the same relationship spoken of in the original covenant with Abraham and his offspring. It is the same covenant God offered to Israel at Mount Sinai. It is the same covenant that God desires to make with us today. How awesome!

Stopping at Mount Sinai is a vital part of our journey to having God as our King. It is the perfect time and place to enter into a covenantal relationship with God. Why? God wants to establish this covenant only after we have experienced *Him*. He allows for time to let us get to know Him. Israel followed, and experienced, God for three months before He asked them into this relationship. He does this because He doesn't want us to enter into this relationship with doubts and hesitation. Nor does He want us to "settle" with Him as our God. He wants us to see His unfailing love for us so we will truly love Him in return. He gives us plenty of opportunities to see who He is—what it would be like to have Him as our God—so we will enter into this covenant with confidence. Then, once we are ready to make this covenantal relationship official, God reveals the terms of the covenant.

Every covenant has terms. What is God asking from us in this relationship? What does God promise to us as His part in this?

The Israelites gathered at the base of the mountain and listened as God spoke the conditions. He began by reminding the Israelites why they would want to enter into this covenant with Him. He brought back to their memories the first part of the journey, as well as who He is and what He does. "I am the LORD your God, who brought you out of the land of Egypt, out of the house of slavery" (Exodus 20:2).

For His part, He would be their God, with all of what that entails: unfailing love, amazing grace, immeasurable mercy, unending faithfulness, and complete rescue and salvation. He would be their Creator, Redeemer, Healer, Comforter, High Priest, Counselor, Savior, and Father. He would take care of them. He would change them into the best they could be. He would give them life *more abundant*. He was promising that He, the Lord— the Great I AM, the Almighty God, the Creator of the Universe— would be *their* God. This is also, by the way, exactly what He is promising to each one of us who enters into this relationship.

What would Israel's part be? What followed was what God said they would do, or how they would act, if they really loved Him. This is *our* part of the agreement.

The first four items in the covenantal terms deal with how we will treat Him. First, God says that we will have no other gods before Him (Exodus 20:3). God asks us to be faithful to Him. This shouldn't surprise us. This *is* a relationship covenant. It is the same as asking in a marriage covenant not to have other wives or husbands. God is no different. He doesn't want to compete for our love. In order to love God with all that we are— our heart, mind, and soul—our first priority, our only allegiance, and our greatest love should be toward God. If He is to be our God we cannot chase after other gods. When we enter into this relationship with God we will be faithful to Him.

Next, He says that we will not make any idols or worship them (Exodus 20:4–6). Idols were not simply a painting or a sculpture of a god, but *the god itself* to the people. Thus, God is asking us not to "make" anything, or allow anything, to take His place in our lives. Idols steal our worship and rule our lives—whether it is money, a symbol, or an admired human (even another Christian). We can even get to the point where we think that *we* are God's greatest example to mankind, pushing the only perfect example, Jesus, aside. But, our covenant with God says that we will not allow any created thing to replace Him, or what He does, in our lives, and therefore take our worship and service from Him.

Then, God says that we will not take His name in vain (Exodus 20:7). Most often this is simplified to mean "don't swear," but it goes much deeper than removing foul language. A more literal way to translate this would be, "do not take my name upon your-selves in emptiness." More than merely forbidding the misuse of God's name in your speech, this focuses on the improper representation of God's name *in your life*. In other words, don't call yourself God's and not live like He asks. It is like a woman who, shortly after shouting and cussing at people while driving in traffic, was pulled over. After a few questions, though, she was released. Infuriated, she demanded to know why she was pulled over. The officer answered, "I noticed the Christian bumper sticker on the car and saw how you were acting, and I assumed the car was stolen."

This is the part of the covenant where God says to honor His name—represent His character well. By becoming His, we are taking His name upon ourselves. It is similar to taking on a last name in a marriage. When we are unwilling to forgive, what does that say about the God we represent? When we are un-loving or lack mercy, what kind of reputation are we giving God's name? How many times do we, who claim to follow Christ, not act Christ-like? 2 Timothy 3:5 describes such people as "having the appearance of godliness, but denying its power." These are those who talk the talk but don't walk the walk—representing God with an empty life. However, this covenant says that after we enter into this relationship with God, we will live in such a way as to keep His name holy and honorable.

Finally, God says that, as His people, we will remember His Sabbath by keeping it holy (Exodus 20:8-11). God adds that our part of the covenant (in how we treat Him) includes remembering to meet with Him on His special day, the Sabbath. Sadly, far too many think that this one is negotiable—that any day can substitute the one He made holy (Genesis 2:1-3). Yet, if we love God with all our heart, mind, and soul we will look forward to meeting with Him on *His* day.† In fact, we will do everything we can to make sure we spend the whole day with Him—not just one or two hours—because in this covenant He is our God and we love Him and want to spend time with Him. When we enter into this relationship with God, we will desire to remember which day is holy and special *to Him* and we'll keep it that way.

As we enter into this covenant with God, He asks us to put aside our kingdom and seek His. He asks that we love Him above all else. He asks that we follow and obey Him. But that's not all. Our covenant with God will also affect how we treat each other.

---

† It is beyond the scope of this book to fully discuss which day is the Biblical Sabbath. However, I wish to offer this brief explanation. According to the commandment (Exodus 20:10), God says the seventh day is His Sabbath. He connects this with the creation story, which says that when God made the seventh day, He rested on it, blessed it, and made it holy (see Genesis 2:1-3). Some suggest that the Sabbath was just for the Jews. However, since it was part of creation (even before sin), it existed long before the Hebrew nation was formed. Therefore, we can know, as Jesus said, that the Sabbath was made for everyone (Mark 2:27). In addition, there was no change in which day was Sabbath (the seventh) from creation to the giving of the law at Mount Sinai. Nor was there change in the day from Mount Sinai to when Jesus walked on this earth. Since Jesus did not make a change to the day (He kept it, in fact—see Luke 4:16), nor did He authorize such a change (the Apostles kept the Sabbath after the resurrection and Jesus' ascension—see Acts 17:2), God's Sabbath would still be the seventh day of the week today.

He continues the terms by telling us to honor our parents (Exodus 20:12). This isn't a command to mindless obedience; God says we are to honor them. It literally means: give them weight in your life. Yes, we are to obey our parents, but this is more about *valuing* our parents; it means treating them with honor their whole life. Treating them how you would want to be treated when you get to their age. Notice, though, that there is no clause about getting off the hook if you didn't get the best parents. As you will see, valuing others, regardless of how they treat you, is the core of the second half of our covenant with God—and God begins with our parents.

Next, God says we will not murder (Exodus 20:13). In His teachings, Jesus reminded us that this is not limited to the actual taking of a life. He said that anger and hate are judged the same as murder (Matthew 5:21, 22). We can "murder" a person's self-esteem, reputation, and salvation by hate alone. But when we enter into a covenant with God we are agreeing to value other people's lives, in every aspect, as much as we value our own.

In addition, in this covenant, we will not commit adultery (Exodus 20:14). Once again, this is not speaking only about purity of the marriage bed, but also purity of thoughts. Jesus explained that if we look upon another person in a covetous way we have already committed adultery (Matthew 5:27, 28). This principle is about not allowing, or wanting, someone else to take the place of your spouse, in *any* area of your marriage. Avoiding these actions and thoughts not only shows respect to the spouse but also to the other person. When we enter into a relationship with God, we will value our spouse and stay pure and true to them in every way.

We will not steal either (Exodus 20:15). We are not to take something that is not our own. This would include taking the credit for something you didn't do, or finding a questionable loophole so you can cheat someone out of something that is theirs. Just think of it this way: how do you feel when someone cheats you out of something you've earned or purchased? Our covenant with God says that we will value other people's right to what is theirs.

Then, God tells us not to give a false testimony (Exodus 20:16). We all know the damage that a lie can do, but this is much more than a lie; it is about giving a testimony that is *deceptive*. It isn't simply a matter of true or false—even truth can be used to mislead. This is about harming the person with what we say about them. Consider gossip: it is deceptive testimony at its worst. Gossip often has just enough truth yet is absent of love, making it very damaging. As people in a relationship with God, our love for others will make us careful that our testimony of them is not deceptive or harmful.

Finally, God says we will not covet (Exodus 20:17). This is just as much about contentment with what we have as it is about wishing we had what others have. In other words, we are to value what God gives us, and find fulfillment in it. If we do not have what the Jones' have, it's okay. God may choose to bless them differently than us. He knows what we each need and wants to pour blessings upon each one of us. Not appreciating what God gives us can easily lead to breaking another part of our covenant with Him. A part of being in a relationship with God is being grateful for what He's given us while also being happy for the blessings He gives to others.

These are six principles that govern our interaction with each other, and the core of each is about how we value, or love, one another. "By this all people will know that you are my disciples, if you have love for one another" (John 13:35).

Not long after God frees you from your Egypt, and before you enter into Canaan, He will bring you to Sinai. He stops to ask you the most important question of this journey: *will you be His?* God will only ask you this when you have already experienced His love, care, and protection. By this point in your journey, you know the kind of God He is.

Friend, you do not have to wait until Canaan to be His. In fact, God cannot be King of your life if you will not enter into this covenant. That is why God proposes here at the foot of the mountain. He wants to start an official relationship right now. Full dependence on Him will come, but right now, He is simply asking if you want Him to be *your* God. He's asking if you will be His. If you will agree to this new relationship, He asks that you love Him with everything you have and are, and that you show love to others as He has shown love to you.

The Creator of the Universe, the God who rescued you from sin, has just popped the question to you. So, right now in this moment—at your Mount Sinai—you have a choice to make. Will you be His? Will you let Him be *your* God?

> "Therefore he is the mediator of a new covenant, so that those who are called may receive the promised eternal inheritance, since a death has occurred that redeems them from the transgressions committed under the first covenant."
>
> HEBREWS 9:15

CHAPTER 6

GETTING THE BEST DEAL

Have you ever entered into a contract and immediately regretted it? Maybe you didn't read the fine print and only after signing did you realize what you had gotten into. Like that time your family bought that time-share property in Egypt only to learn that you were trapped in a contract requiring you to build your own bricks, *without* straw or clay. Now *that* was buyers' remorse! Perhaps you have been misled by the grand promises of a sales person. Like the time you bought that new-for-you camel from *Crazy Ishmael's Discount Camels and Donkeys*. His sales pitch was slick—it sounded too good to be true… and it was. Sure, it was the latest model, but you never had anything but trouble from it, and its third hump was definitely *not* a premium feature.

Because such experiences are common (okay, maybe not those *specific* ones), you may have some apprehensions entering into any contract or covenant too quickly. Therefore, since the Promised Land charter bus has pulled into a campsite to remain around

Sinai for a little while, I want to spend a little more time on the choice presented in the last chapter.

Entering into a covenantal relationship with God is the most important decision you will ever make. Therefore, you will want to make sure you are entering into the best covenant possible, and it doesn't take an Old Testament attorney to see that the covenant God made with Israel at Mount Sinai is, well, *old*. *Really* old. It is often considered restrictive and obsolete. Why would anyone today want to enter into such an out-dated covenant? Is there a fresh, new-and-improved covenant for followers of God today?

Actually, there is. Jesus Himself said so. Just hours before He faced the crucifixion, He shared the Passover meal with His disciples (Luke 22:15). During that meal, He took symbols that pointed to Israel's exodus from Egypt and repurposed them to remind His disciples of the sacrifice He was about to offer. The next time they would have this meal, He wanted them to think of Him and what He did. Just as the bread was broken during the meal, it would later remind them that His body was broken for them. Then He gave them His cup to drink. After they drank it, He said, "This is my blood of the covenant, which is poured out for many" (Mark 14:23, 24). In Luke's gospel, Jesus' statement is a little different: "This cup that is poured out for you is the *new covenant* in my blood" (Luke 22:20, emphasis mine). This would remind them—and us, as we still celebrate the Lord's Supper—of His blood that was shed, and that they were entering into a *new* covenant with Him. So it is true, in Jesus' own words: there is a new covenant for us.

Now, it is easy to assume that since the covenant is new, everything is different. However, notice the language of this new covenant when it was promised by God in the book of Jeremiah.

> Behold, the days are coming, declares the LORD, when I
> will make a new covenant with the house of Israel and

the house of Judah, not like the covenant that I made with their fathers on the day when I took them by the hand to bring them out of the land of Egypt, my covenant that they broke, though I was their husband, declares the LORD. For this is the covenant that I will make with the house of Israel after those days, declares the LORD: I will put my law within them, and I will write it on their hearts. And I will be their God, and they shall be my people. (Jeremiah 31:31–33)

In this promise, we see that the new covenant has the same relationship-based language as the old covenant: God would be our God, and we would be His people. If the language of the covenant is still the same, what else is the same between the old and the new? How much is different? Interestingly, not that much is different between the two.

For instance, in the very beginning—the first mention of the covenant made with Abraham—God established that one of Abraham's (and his descendants') requirements for the covenant was circumcision. Many today believe that this requirement is no longer relevant. Yet notice what Colossians 2:11 says: "In him also you were circumcised with a circumcision made without hands, by putting off the body of the flesh, by the circumcision of Christ."

Paul says that there still is a requirement of circumcision—just not the kind we assume. He describes the "new" idea of this requirement more clearly in his letter to the Romans: "For no one is a Jew who is merely one outwardly, nor is circumcision outward and physical. But a *Jew is one inwardly, and circumcision is a matter of the heart,* by the spirit, not by the letter" (Romans 2:28, 29, emphasis mine). To Paul, true circumcision is inward—a matter of the heart. It may be hard to believe, but this is what God truly desired in the old covenant. Consider these passages:

"Circumcise therefore the foreskin of your heart, and be no longer stubborn." (Deuteronomy 10:16)

"And the LORD your God will circumcise your heart and the heart of your offspring, so that you will love the LORD your God with all your heart and with all your soul, that you may live." (Deuteronomy 30:6)

"Circumcise yourselves to the LORD; remove the foreskin of your hearts . . . ." (Jeremiah 4:4)

"Behold, the days are coming, declares the LORD, when I will punish all those who are circumcised merely in the flesh . . . all the house of Israel are uncircumcised in heart." (Jeremiah 9:25, 26)

God has always wanted His people to be circumcised in the heart—removing the selfishness and stubbornness in our lives—resulting in our loving Him with all of our heart and soul. So, the requirement of circumcision hasn't changed.

Of course, I found that in most theological discussions, the one thing consistently brought up as being done away with in the new covenant is the Ten Commandments. Typically, the argument is made that the law was nailed to the cross and we are no longer under the law, but under grace.

First, it is true that the Ten Commandments were part of the old covenant—as we learned in the last chapter, they spell out the terms of the relationship. However, in the promise of a new covenant (Jeremiah 31:31–33) we find the first crack in the foundation of that argument: it does not mention that the new covenant will do away with God's Law, replacing it with grace; instead, God says, "I will put my law *within* them, and I will write it *on their hearts*" (Jeremiah 31:33, emphasis mine). The new covenant does not remove the law. If anything, the law will become more a part of us. Instead of being written on stones kept inside an ark that few people ever see, God desires to write His covenantal law *inside* us—keeping the law will become something *we want to do.*

Of course, this doesn't explain the verse that says that the law was nailed to the cross. Many use this text to suggest that Jesus' sacrifice did away with the law. However, under such logic, if someone paid everyone's speeding tickets then every speed limit would be removed. Yeah, we wish! We know that is not the case. It is also not true of this passage.

The text in question is Colossians 2:14: "[B]y canceling the record of debt that stood against us with its legal demands. This he set aside, nailing it to the cross." Interestingly, the verse does not say that the law was nailed to the cross, but that "the record of debt" that stood against us was nailed to the cross. The Greek word translated as "record" describes a handwritten statement, especially a record of financial accounts. According to the original language of the text, what was nailed to the cross was our debts and its legal demands (see Romans 6:23)—the things that really stand against us—not the law. This makes more sense. Christ's sacrifice for our sins could only cancel our debt (payment for sin) and would not cancel out the law (which *reveals* sin—see Romans 7:7). The penalty was removed, not the law.

Still, aren't we now under grace and not the law? "For sin will have no dominion over you, since you are not under law but under grace" (Romans 6:14). This is a beautiful passage about the power of grace over sin; however, it does not say that the law has been done away with—it only says that we are no longer *under* it. Plus, we cannot ignore the very next verse: "What then? Are we to sin because we are not under law but under grace? By no means!" (Romans 6:15). In fact, an honest reading of Paul's letters would reveal that, although we are not saved by keeping the law, the law still stands: "Do we then overthrow the law by this faith? By no means! On the contrary, we uphold the law" (Romans 3:31; see also Galatians 3:17–19).

Besides, if Christ's death on the cross got rid of the law, why would He say, "Do not think that I have come to abolish the Law or the Prophets; *I have not come to abolish them but to fulfill them*" (Matthew 5:17—emphasis mine)? Or, why would He say, "If you love me, you will keep my commandments" (John 14:15)? In Jesus' own words, He did not abolish or remove the Law, but fulfilled it through His own actions, and before going to the cross, asked us to continue keeping it.

John's teachings (which were written years after the cross) also contradict the idea that the law was gone: "And by this we know that we have come to know him, if we keep his commandments. Whoever says 'I know him' but does not keep his commandments is a liar, and the truth is not in him" (1 John 2:3, 4). Furthermore, He wrote that when we love God we will keep His commandments and "his commandments are not burdensome." (1 John 5:2, 3).

Finally, if the law was gone and no longer part of the new covenant, then why are the end-time people of God described as those "who keep the commandments of God" (see Revelation 12:17 and 14:12)?

No, Jesus' sacrifice did not remove the law, it paid the debt that the law reveals in our lives. Therefore, the new covenant has not changed the law either—it still stands. Again, this makes sense. A covenant always includes the conditions for both parties. In both the old and new covenant, God's part is being our God; He will protect us and is saving us. Likewise, our part is still loving Him with all our heart (circumcision of the heart) and following Him (obedience). The new covenant did not change this.

So far, quite a bit of the new covenant is the same as the old covenant. Not as much has changed as many today have claimed.

Of course, God did say, "I will not violate my covenant or alter the word that went forth from my lips" (Psalm 89:34).

However, there *is* a new covenant. This implies something is different. And there is a difference.

There is one aspect of the former covenant that was changed, though not removed, in the new covenant. Our first hint is in Jesus' statement that the new covenant would be "in His blood" (Luke 22:20; Matthew 26:28; Mark 14:24). Thus, in search of the answer to what is new about the covenant, we need to look into the change His blood brings. For this, we go to an interesting passage in Exodus:

> Then [Moses] took the Book of the Covenant and read it in the hearing of the people. And they said, "All that the LORD has spoken we will do, and we will be obedient." And Moses took the blood [from the animal sacrifice—see verses 5, 6] and threw it on the people and said, "Behold *the blood of the covenant* that the LORD has made with you in accordance to all these words." (Exodus 24:7, 8, notes and emphasis mine)

According to this passage, one of the aspects of the covenant made with Israel was that it was inaugurated through the blood of animals. We find this same idea written in Hebrews 9:18–22, where the author makes the concluding statement that "without the shedding of blood there is no forgiveness of sins." It is no coincidence that, at the beginning of the old covenant as well as the start of the new covenant, there is mention of the "blood of the covenant." In the old covenant, it was the blood of animals. Therefore, it is Jesus' blood that makes the new covenant new.

This change was prophesied long ago. Messianic prophecies found in Isaiah 42:6 and 49:8 say that the Messiah would be given "as a covenant for the people." In other words, Jesus, the Messiah, would become the covenant to us. Another interesting messianic prophecy is found in Daniel 9:27. It says that the Messiah would confirm a covenant with many for one week, and in the middle of that week, He would put an end to sacrifice and offering. Due to the symbolic language in prophecy this may seem confusing at first, but the major theme of this prophecy should become clearer as we look at what Jesus did.

Jesus made it clear that the Last Supper was to symbolize His broken body and shed blood, and that it would all point to the cross. But how does this change the covenants?

As we learned, the blood of animals (as a sacrifice) was needed during the old covenant. In fact, the whole sacrificial system, including the priesthood, was required for forgiveness under that covenant (more on this in the next chapter). The priests would mediate on behalf of the people by offering their sacrifices before God inside the Holy Place of the Sanctuary. However, that system had a serious flaw. Besides the fact that God promised to make a new covenant (Jeremiah 31:31–34), the old system was mediated by men who were temporary (they died) and imperfect (they sinned), and it was paid by insufficient blood (an animal's blood, which cannot pay man's debt of sin).

Then Jesus died... and everything changed.

When He died, the curtain in the Temple (that separated the Holy and Most Holy Places) was torn in two from top to bottom (Matthew 27:51). This miracle interrupted the sacrifices, just for a moment, because a greater sacrifice had taken place. Jesus did not die because of His sin; He died for *our* sin (Isaiah 53:5). *He became the sacrifice for us.*

Instead of relying on the blood of animals, Jesus presents His own blood as payment—and for a good reason:

> He entered once for all into the holy places, not by means
> of the blood of goats and calves but by means of his own

blood, thus securing an eternal redemption. For if the blood of goats and bulls, and the sprinkling of defiled persons with the ashes of a heifer, sanctify for the purification of the flesh, how much more will the blood of Christ, who through the eternal Spirit offered himself without blemish to God, purify our conscience from dead works to serve the living God. Therefore he is the mediator of a new covenant, so that those who are called may receive the promised eternal inheritance, since a death has occurred that redeems them from the transgressions committed under the first covenant. (Hebrews 9:12–15)

Not only did Jesus become the payment of the new covenant, but also the mediator. Psalms 110:4 (another messianic prophecy) says that Jesus would be "a priest forever." As a result of Jesus' sacrifice—and resurrection—all of the flaws of the old covenant were covered. As Hebrews 7:23–25 says,

The former priests were many in number, because they were prevented by death from continuing in office, but he holds his priesthood permanently, because he continues forever. Consequently, he is able to save to the uttermost those who draw dear to God through him, since he always lives to make intercession for them.

This is the new covenant in Jesus: His sacrifice and priesthood makes the first one obsolete (Hebrews 8:13). No longer do we need to sacrifice animals for our sins—Jesus paid it all! No longer do we need a human priest to mediate on our behalf— Jesus is our High Priest! He ended the need for sacrifices and offerings by becoming the offering. This is what makes the new covenant new. It's what makes the new covenant better. We have a better Payment and a better Priest.

Remember, when Israel entered into the covenant with God in Exodus 24, Moses poured the blood on the people. They started their relationship covered in the "blood of the covenant." This is still a requirement of the covenant. However, now, after the cross, we start our relationship with God covered completely by the blood of Jesus.

Yes, there is a new covenant and it is much better. Today, if you choose to enter into a relationship with God, it will be under this new, and far superior, covenant. It is not better because it has done away with all the rules and requirements—because when you love God, His commands are not burdensome (John 14:15; 1 John 5:3). It is better because it is one hundred percent effective. Because Jesus' sacrifice can cover *every* sin—those committed under the new *and* the old covenants. Because Jesus becomes your Sacrifice, your Savior, and your Mediator. The new covenant in Jesus' blood is greater because it is the only way eternal life is possible. Praise God for the new covenant!

"As God said, 'I will make my dwelling among them and walk among them, and I will be their God, and they shall be my people.'"

2 CORINTHIANS 6:16

CHAPTER 7

WHEN GOD MOVES IN

Some people have the gift, some don't. You can tell those who do as soon as you enter their house. It is the gift of interior decoration. It is not necessarily easy to decorate well. Just ask anyone who has been asked to put a picture "over there . . . no over there. Hmm . . . no, go back to where you first had it." In an attempt to help, there are books sold that are designed to make your home a palace, or at least allow you to imagine your house is a palace. In addition, from small home decorating shows by certain celebrities to complete home makeovers, even television is spreading the joy.

To those in the know, every piece of furniture is put in its place for a reason; everything has its purpose. Of course, there are those who may just throw some furniture in a room and accept it where it lands. I'm guessing that most of you would not do that. Neither would God.

While camped at Sinai, God gave the Israelites another gift. After entering into this new relationship with them, He made it known that He would move in with them. The Creator of the Universe would live among His people. He revealed the plans for His new dwelling place—His tent or, as it would be called, the Tabernacle. It would also be the place where they would come to worship and give gifts of gratitude to Him.

The Israelites were more than happy to build the Tabernacle for God. Yet, its significance is much greater than just a place for Him to live. To understand, we need to go back in time a bit further.

Immediately after the Fall, before any Hebrew existed, God had set in motion His plan for the salvation of mankind. From that moment, lambs were sacrificed for sins in a simple ceremony that looked forward in faith to the full solution of God's plan (Genesis 4:4). However, while slaves in Egypt, God's people had forgotten about His plan. Therefore, after they were freed from slavery, God needed to reintroduce His Plan of Salvation to them. He did this through the Tabernacle and its services.

This is also the significance of the Tabernacle for us: it can help us better understand Christ's complete redemptive work in our lives. It is an object lesson that lays out salvation for us. Thus, the better we understand the Sanctuary, the better we'll understand what God is doing for our salvation. The clearer we see God's plan the more we'll understand His love for us and, as a result, fall more in love with Him.

A brief look at the design of the Tabernacle, the Sanctuary (the main structure inside), and its furniture will reveal that everything had a purpose and a meaning. Not one part of the design was by chance. We are told in Hebrews 8:5 that the earthly sanctuary is a copy, or a "shadow" of what is in Heaven. In other words, the place the Israelites built at Sinai is modeled after God's true dwelling place in Heaven.

It is also important to note that when God gave Israel the blueprints He also gave them instructions on how it was to be built and who would built it. God didn't tell them to find the cheapest bid. He told them to use bronze and gold and luxurious colors and fabric. He personally picked out the people who would work on each part—each one known for their excellence in their craft. Why? Because God doesn't want average, or just okay. He wants the best—the best materials and the best workers. Sadly, we often give God our leftovers. We should always give God our best. Of course, since this would be a shadow of His true dwelling place in Heaven, it had to be the best possible representation.

So, while we are still here at Sinai, let's take a tour of God's Tabernacle and consider its wonderful design.*

Even before we enter, we should take notice that the walls of the courtyard are half the height of the Sanctuary. This was done so people could see the Sanctuary's golden walls and beautiful coverings even outside of the courtyard.

There is only one entrance into the Tabernacle and it is in the east wall. This was unusual for a place of worship in Israel's time. Every other religion entered from the west, facing east and the rising sun. This was significant because they worshipped the sun. However, when we are in a relationship with God, we will not bow down or worship anything else. So God had His people enter from the east, with their backs to the sun, when they worshipped Him so they could focus on Him.

Upon entering, we find ourselves in the courtyard (Exodus 27:9–19), which is twice as long as it is wide (about 150 feet long by 75 feet wide). The courtyard is beautiful, yet ordinary. Everything in the courtyard is made of brass, a beautiful yet common metal. This is the place where common people were allowed. In fact, this was as far as anyone other than a priest could go. Even so, once inside the courtyard, besides seeing the whole sanctuary in all of its glory and a congregation of people participating in faith, our eyes fall on the first major object.

---

* This is not intended to be an exhaustive examination of the sanctuary, but will hopefully reveal the beauty of these "shadows" and create in you a desire to study it further. Its description can be found in Exodus 25–27, 30, and 36–38.

Positioned between the courtyard entrance and the entrance to the Tabernacle is the altar of burnt offerings (Exodus 27:1–8; 40:6). Don't miss this! The very first thing inside is the altar. Before we get to the presence of God, the altar is needed. This altar of brass is about seven and a half feet square. It was here that all of the sacrifices—all of the burnt offerings—were made. No sacrifice ever took place further inside the sanctuary, only in the courtyard. This, in a way, alludes to the idea that the earth is the "courtyard" of the Heavenly Sanctuary, since the earth is where the ultimate sacrifice took place.

This was a very busy location in the tabernacle. Every morning and evening (before they started the day and as they ended the day) the people made sure they were right with God by offering a sacrifice for their sins. It is no surprise, then, when Jesus said that we must take up our cross daily and follow Him (Luke 9:23). Once again, do not overlook the importance of the fact that the first thing in the sanctuary focuses on repentance and sacrifice.

As we pass the brass altar, we come to the laver or wash basin located between the altar and the Sanctuary entrance (Exodus 30:17–21). Here, the priests washed their hands and feet before they entered into the Sanctuary. This was very important. If they entered into the sanctuary without doing this, they would die. God does not take it lightly when holy things are treated as common. So before a priest could enter into the holier areas, they needed to clean themselves from the common area. It is similar to the concept in Jesus' statement about baptism, that "unless one is born of water and the Spirit, he cannot enter the kingdom of God" (John 3:5). Like the priests, before we can ever enter into God's presence, we too need to be washed and made clean.

This would be as far as the average person could go. Only the priests entered past this point. Most people would never see inside the Sanctuary. However, for the sake of having a complete tour, we will pretend that we are priests in Israel and continue inside, into the Holy Place. Just inside, on our left (south), we see the golden lampstand (Exodus 25:31–37). Notice the change in material. There isn't a section of silver—it goes from brass to gold. Inside the Sanctuary, only the most precious metal is used. Not only is the lampstand gold, but it also has seven branches made of gold that are beaten into intricate shapes of flowers and buds. On each of these branches are lamps that burn before the Lord continually (Leviticus 24:2, 3).

Other religions blew out the lamps at night because their gods needed sleep. A great example happened during the show-down between Elijah and the priests of Baal. He challenged them to shout louder because, perhaps, Baal was asleep (1 Kings 18:27). Their reaction was to shout even louder—they thought it was possible! However, since the lamps in the Holy Place burn all night, it reveals to everyone (including the other nations) that *our God never sleeps.*

Every morning and evening (during the morning and evening sacrifices) the priests trim and light the lamps (Exodus 30:7, 8). We find a significant parallel in Revelation 1:12–20, where John saw Jesus walking among the seven lamp stands. Jesus explained that the lamps represented churches. Since the number seven in the Bible represents completion, this would represent Christ's complete church, His people. His people, then, would need to be regularly trimmed and re-lit so their lights could always shine brightly. Furthermore, in Zechariah 4:1–14, we learn that the lamp and the oil is the combination of God's Spirit and His Word that creates a light in us. Thus, every single day we should be trimmed and lit by the Holy Spirit and the Word of God.

Next, if we turn around in the room, facing north, we see the table of the bread of the Presence (Exodus 25:23–30). It is about three feet long, one and a half feet wide, two and a quarter feet high and is made of acacia wood overlaid with gold. On this table are twelve loaves of bread in two piles, six in a pile (Leviticus 24:5, 6). These loaves were made every Sabbath and placed on the table hot. The bread would remain there all week long and then the priests would eat it the following Sabbath. Interestingly, after the Israelites entered into Canaan and would make regular bread for physical nourishment, it was to be prepared *before* the Sabbath. However, the Bread of the Presence was special—it was to be made, and enjoyed, *on* the Sabbath. Again, we are reminded of something Jesus said about Himself: He is the Bread of Life, sent from God (John 6:51–53). What a wonderful symbol of the special communion God wants to have with us on the Sabbath.

Furthermore, since the bread stayed on the table all week, other nations could see that *our God does not depend on us for nourishment* (like other "gods"); but rather, it was a constant reminder of our dependence on Him. God does not need our bread, but we need His bread. God was not created by us and is not sustained by us. He does not need us for survival. We need *Him*.

Turning away from the entrance we'll see the veil dividing us from the Most Holy Place. In front of the veil is the altar of incense (Exodus 30:1–10). It is a smaller altar—about one and a half feet square and three feet high. It is also made of acacia wood and entirely overlaid in gold. But, not just anything can be burned here. Only incense is allowed, and even then, it is a special, sacred recipe given to Israel by God. The formula was so sacred that anyone found using the formula for anything else would be cut off from the people. Since the recipe could not be used anywhere else, this unique aroma became tied to the sanctuary. I'm sure you can understand this significance. Have you ever been brought back to a childhood memory because of a certain smell? Like the smell of freshly baked bread that Grandma used to make, or the fragrance of a flower that grew near your house. Or perhaps you knew you were close to your destination because of a specific aroma? That happened to my family when we lived in

Amarillo, Texas. We knew we were getting close to home when we started to smell the feedlots (that was *not* sweet-smelling incense though). For the Israelites, this special scent let them know they were nearing the sanctuary and reminded them of the sacrifice and forgiveness that happened there.

This sacred incense was also renewed every morning and evening so the incense would be constantly burning before the Lord (Exodus 30:8). In fact, it was done at the same time as the trimming of the lamps. Once again, we find a similar image in Revelation 8:3, 4: John saw the altar in Heaven and the incense was mixed with the prayer of the saints. The special incense was necessary to present the prayers before God. The incense always burning not only reveals a God who always hears, but also unveils the work of the Holy Spirit, who intercedes for us when we pray with "groanings too deep for words" (Romans 8:26, 27). The Holy Spirit is the sacred ingredient. God's Spirit is the sweet fragrance of our prayers. And the altar of incense represents a continual, daily intercession before God with the help of the Holy Spirit.

This was as far as the regular priest could go. Only the High Priest could continue past the veil and go into the Most Holy Place, and only on one specific day of the year.[†] If they entered any other time of the year, they would die (Leviticus 16:2). God does not take it lightly when humanity desecrates His holy things. This room was so sacred that, even when the High Priest could enter, he would tie a rope around his waist and bells on his garments so that if he did anything to defile the Most Holy Place and died, he could be pulled out. No one would dare go in after him.

Of course, it is called the *Most* Holy Place for a reason. For inside this room is the most important and most beautiful object of the whole sanctuary: the ark of the covenant (Exodus 25:10–22). Words fail to describe what is seen. The ark was a little over

---

† The High Priest only entered into the Most Holy Place during the annual feast on the Day of Atonement (see Leviticus 16:1–34 for the description of this feast).

three and a half feet long and two and a quarter feet wide and high. It was also made of acacia wood overlaid with gold. By Solomon's day, the only things inside the ark were the two stone tablets of the Law (1 Kings 8:9). But it's not the container that holds your attention—it is the cover. It is made of pure gold, with two excellently crafted cherubim at each end of the cover, their wings spread upward, overshadowing it. Facing each other, they look toward the center where God's presence—His glory—shines. This is where the Hight Priests meet with God. It is where atonement takes place. Best of all, it is called the mercy seat.

Stop for a moment and think about this: God covers His law with a mercy seat! It is here that the peoples' sins are ultimately brought and forgiveness takes place. This cover represents no other place than God's throne! There is no question that this is the center of the whole sanctuary. Yes, in God's kingdom there is a law, but His throne is a throne of mercy! This is significant. As the author of Hebrews wrote:

> Since then we have a great high priest who has passed through the heavens, Jesus, the Son of God, let us hold fast our confession. For we do not have a high priest who is unable to sympathize with our weaknesses, but one who in every respect has been tempted as we are, yet without sin. Let us then with confidence draw near to the throne of grace, that we may receive mercy and find grace to help in time of need. (Hebrews 4:14–16)

God's throne is a throne of grace—a mercy seat—because Jesus is our High Priest. Sometimes we think that God does not understand what we are going through. We feel as though the temptations in our lives are greater than God can comprehend. This passage reminds us that Jesus was tempted in every way that we are (maybe not with the exact same things, but in the same respect). For that reason, Jesus *does* understand what we are going through and sympathizes with us. The difference is that, though He was tempted, He had victory over sin. It is His victory in righteousness that allows for mercy. It is His sinless life that provides the opportunity for grace.

This is why God wants to move in with you. Living with you moves His throne of grace into your life. It has always been a part of His plan: "As God said, 'I will make my dwelling among them and walk among them, and I will be their God, and they shall be my people'" (2 Corinthians 6:16). He wants to live with you and walk with you. You don't have to build a tabernacle with brass, gold, and acacia wood though. He desires a new temple: "For we are the temple of the living God" (2 Corinthians 6:16); "Do you not know that *you are God's temple* and that God's Spirit dwells in you?" (1 Corinthians 3:16, emphasis mine).

You've already seen that God wants to write His law in your heart (Jeremiah 31:33), but now He wants to move His throne there as well. It isn't an easy decision either, because your heart is the location of *your* throne. What He's basically asking is to exchange your throne for His.

The tabernacle, sanctuary, and every item inside is a wonderful object lesson of His plan for your salvation. It is an example of His complete makeover for your life. This is what the journey through the sanctuary is all about: entering as a sinful slave, and leaving redeemed and forgiven. From the daily sacrifice for your sin to allowing Christ to "trim" you, causing your light to shine brighter. From being washed clean to sending up prayers before a God who always hears. Ultimately, you'll end up standing before the mercy seat; the place where you will meet with God; the place where you will find forgiveness and atonement. It is His throne—His eternal presence—in your life.

Will you accept this gift and allow God to move His throne of grace into your heart right now?

"And you, who were dead in your trespasses and the uncircumcision of your flesh, God made alive together with him, having forgiven us all our trespasses, by canceling the record of debt that stood against us with its legal demands. This he set aside, nailing it to the cross."

COLOSSIANS 2:13, 14

CHAPTER 8

GETTiNG OUT OF DEBT

In the late 1990s, LendingTree (an online lending marketplace) debuted a commercial about a man named Stanley Johnson. In the advertisement, Stanley talks to the camera about the wonderful things in his life: his great family and his four-bedroom house in a great community. He happily points out his new car and proudly reveals that he even belongs to the local golf club. Then he asks the question he assumes the listener wants to know: "How did I do it?" While cleaning his pool, he looks at the camera with a smile on his face and says, "I'm in debt up to my eyeballs!" He then whispers, "I can barely pay my finance charges. Somebody help me!"

While it is meant to be funny, the commercial (ironically from a company that *lends money*) reveals a serious problem in many households: major debt. Many have fallen into the trap of this long-term payoff concept. If we can have it now and pay for it over time, we get excited. Debt is even seen as a necessity by many these days. In fact, as of the writing of this book, the average consumer debt in the United States is $90,460.* Of course debt is not evil all by itself—sometimes it can be necessary—but we often don't think about the real cost of debt. What *is* the real cost of debt, especially substantial debt? It's not just a dollar amount. The real cost is much more. It requires not only full payment but also a significant change in mindset and lifestyle. The true cost will always demand a sacrifice.

Now, I know what you may be thinking: what does debt have to do with our journey to the Promised Land? When the Israelites left slavery they plundered the Egyptians. It would only be natural to assume that they were still quite rich. However, in reality, they left Egypt with an enormous amount of debt. Only it was not monetary debt they had incurred, it was spiritual debt. They were indebted to God.

How could this be? The Bible tells us that sin puts us into debt spiritually: "The wages of sin is death" (Romans 6:23). What we earn for our sinful life is death. Is death a positive or a negative earning? Would you say it is an investment or a debt? It is debt! Since sin entered our world, our rebellious actions have given us a negative balance in the Bank of Eternal Life. Humanity was in debt long before credit cards were ever invented. Furthermore, according to the Bible, we cannot pay our own debt with our own spirituality. In fact, Isaiah tells us that our "righteous" works are like a polluted garment (Isaiah 64:6). Even our "good" works only put us deeper into this debt! The Israelites could never have worked off their debt to God. Even if they had only been obedient (and they weren't), their spiritual debt was too great. Fortunately, there is good news for the Israelites (and us): another reason God wants to live with us is so that He can help us get out of debt.

Part of the Plan of Redemption that God established even before the Fall is a spiritual debt-repayment plan. It is not a debt-

---

* Statistics for 2019. https://www.bankrate.com/finance/debt/average-american-debt/.

reduction plan—God doesn't forgive only a part of it and have us work off the rest—the debt forgiveness in this plan is *complete*. In Jeremiah 33:8, He says, "I will cleanse them from all the guilt of their sin against me, and I will forgive all the guilt of their sin and rebellion against me." God promises to cleanse and forgive *every* sin—big or small; He will forgive all of our debt against Him. But what makes this plan so final is that He takes it one step further: "I am he who blots out your transgressions for my own sake, and I will not remember your sins" (Isaiah 43:25). God doesn't keep a record of "forgiven sins" on His bedside table so He can quickly grab them and remind us of all the bad things we have done before. He forgives and forgets.

Of course, this kind of debt repayment will cost. We have the unfortunate tendency to think that if something doesn't cost *us* anything, it didn't cost anything. In fact, some people today even call the forgiveness God offers, "cheap grace." At the same time, others believe that, if there is a cost, it isn't that high—as if God covered the cost of our lunch. Just because something didn't cost *you* anything doesn't mean it didn't cost someone something. If you owed ten million dollars in back taxes and someone paid it for you, would you think it didn't cost much? The problem might be that we have underestimated the magnitude of our debt. It is likely that we have misjudged the severity of our sins.

According to the Bible, the cost of the forgiveness of our debt of sin is enormous! This is the reality: "[W]ithout the shedding of blood there is no forgiveness of sins" (Hebrews 9:22). If the wages of our sin is death, then death is needed as payment. If not ours, then whose? Ever since the Fall, sacrifices were offered for the debt of sin. Then, here at Sinai, God re-establishes them to remind His people of the true cost of their redemption. Some of these sacrifices were daily and some were occasional. Some were required while others were voluntary. Yet, each of these offerings meant life—they meant forgiveness and salvation.

However, none of these sacrifices would be enough by themselves; they were never meant to be the solution. Instead, together they pointed to a much greater sacrifice. Hebrews 9:15 tells us that it was Jesus' death on the cross that set His people free from sin under the first covenant. In the Old Testament, God's people offered their sacrifices in faith—looking forward to what Jesus *would do* at the cross. And it took all of the different types to reveal what Christ's one sacrifice would achieve. In order to fully appreciate the wonderful new covenant in Christ's blood—in order to truly understand the extraordinary cost of our debt forgiveness—we need to examine the details of the offerings of the first covenant.

I do not intend to cover every sacrifice, or every one of their features.† I only wish to point out a few of the main offerings, and the lessons we can learn from them. So, we will review five that were part of the sanctuary: the grain offering, the peace offering, the burnt offering, the sin offering, and the guilt offering.

As I mentioned before, every offering required a sacrifice—it always cost the giver something—which is the very definition of an offering in the Old Testament. If what you give to God doesn't cost you anything, it isn't a sacrifice. As David said, "I will not offer burnt offerings to the Lord my God that cost me nothing" (2 Samuel 24:24). An offering always costs the giver something. Most of them required a life: the sacrifice of an animal. However, even in this God made room for grace: in cases where a family could not afford the required animal for their sacrifice, exceptions were made. These exceptions allowed the family to provide a lesser animal, like a dove instead of a lamb, or even flour (see Leviticus 5:7–11 for an example).

There was one sacrifice offered on the altar that didn't require an animal at all: the grain offering (Leviticus 2; 6:14–23). It was an

---

† To read more about the different offerings and festivals of the Old Testament sanctuary, read the book of Leviticus.

offering of bread that was to be given with salt but without leaven. A portion of it would be placed on the altar (given to God) and the remainder would be eaten by the priest (unless he was the offerer). Even though it didn't involve the sacrifice of an animal, it was still very important. It was as holy to God as the sin offering (Leviticus 6:17). In fact, notice the meaning of the salt in the bread: "You shall not let the salt of the covenant with your God be missing from your grain offering" (Leviticus 2:13). This was all about their relationship with God. It had nothing to with the removal of sin; it was an expression of a positive relationship with the Lord—kind of like sharing a meal with God. It was an acknowledgement that God was their sustainer of life.

Is it a surprise that Jesus called Himself the "bread of life" (John 6:35), or that He symbolized the breaking of His body on the cross as the broken bread of the Passover meal (Luke 22:19)? As the Bread of Life, He promises that whoever comes to Him will not hunger or thirst. David likened his desire to know God as a deer panting for water (Psalm 42:1). Because of Jesus, we do not have to hunger or thirst for a relationship with Him. As this offering expressed their positive relationship with God, Jesus' sacrificial life makes this positive relationship possible.

For the rest of the main sacrifices, an animal was required. It also had to be unblemished. A person would never bring a weak, sickly, or blemished animal as an offering to God; it needed to be the best from their flock. Of course, we should always offer God our best! Next, the animal was to be taken to the entrance of the sanctuary. In each case, the individual bringing the offering would first lay his hand on the head of the animal, showing the transfer of ownership to God and identifying whom the sacrifice was for. Then, the offerer would confess his sin, transferring it to the animal. Finally, the offerer would take the animal's life with *his own hands* by cutting its throat while a priest caught the blood in a bowl to be sprinkled on an altar in the sanctuary.

Can you imagine having to do this? Yet, you have—through Jesus' sacrifice. Jesus died for your sins—it was the result of *your* hands: "But he was pierced for our transgressions; he was crushed for our iniquities" (Isaiah 53:5). We might cringe at the thought of having to take an animal's life because of our rebellious actions. How differently would you live if you had to *personally* cut the throat of one of your lambs every time you sinned? Now, imagine that every time you sinned was like taking the hammer from one of the Roman soldiers and pounding the nails further into Jesus' hands. Would that make you want to change the way you live? What a graphic presentation of the cost of our sins! Yet, as we already read, there is no forgiveness of sins without the shedding of blood (Hebrews 9:22).

Among the sacrifices that required an animal was the peace, or fellowship, offering (Leviticus 3; 7:11–21). It was voluntarily presented in thanksgiving or to confirm a vow or contract. The individual was required to eat part of the sacrifice. After taking the animal's life, the priest would sprinkle its blood on the sides of the altar and the fat of the animal would be placed on the altar to burn. The priest was given specific parts of the animal and the rest was given to the one presenting it. This offering shows that our fellowship with God does not have to focus on the negative side of removing sins. Yes, it still costs, but by taking part in the life-giving sacrifice of Christ we can be at peace with God and confirm our covenant with Him.

But, what if we find ourselves not right with God? For this we would turn to the burnt offering (Leviticus 1; 6:8–13). This was the most common sacrifice. It was made for atonement. Like the peace offering, after the animal was killed, the blood was also sprinkled on the sides of the altar. However, this time the *whole* animal (except for the hide) was burned—completely consumed—on the altar. The giver did not participate in the consuming; the whole sacrifice was given to God. Likewise, Jesus was completely consumed on the cross, becoming sin for us, that we might be made right with God (2 Corinthians 5:21).

Of course, there is still the problem of sin. The burnt offering made them right with God, but the debt of sin remained. The sin offering points to the solution (Leviticus 4–5:13; 6:24–30). This sacrifice was not a gift, nor was it voluntary; it was a required payment for an obligation or a debt (sin). This time, after the animal was sacrificed, the blood would be sprinkled on the horns of the altar instead of the sides, revealing the greater importance of the blood of this sacrifice. If a priest or the whole nation sinned, the blood would be sprinkled seven times "before the veil" and then put on the horns of the golden altar of incense as well. Thus, the blood was brought closer to God vertically (on the horns instead of the sides) and closer to His presence (inside the Holy Place). Again we see the parallel in Jesus, our payment for sin, who was also lifted up, with His blood shed high on Calvary.

Finally, there was the guilt offering (Leviticus 5:14–6:7; 7:1–10). This sacrifice atoned for three different circumstances: first, misuse of something holy that belongs to God; second, any unknown sin/ rebellion; third, a false oath that misused God's holy name. Don't miss this. God holds us responsible for our treatment of holy things. Furthermore, the guilt offering revealed our responsibility to our neighbors. For, in addition to the offering at the sanctuary, it required a literal repayment or reparation to the party offended. Why? Remember, our covenant with God also affects our relationships with each other. To continue to be right with God requires that we strive to be right with each other (no, it doesn't always work out, but that doesn't mean we shouldn't try to make amends). I like how one author explains it: "Forgiveness through Christ is not a 'cheap grace' way to declare bankruptcy on our obligations to other people."‡ We must do

---

‡ Roy Gane, *Altar Call* (Berrien Springs, MI: Diadem, 1999), 103.

everything in our power to make things right for those we sin against. If we do this, we are released from the guilt. The beauty of this is that whether or not we know how we've sinned against God or someone else, we can be freed from our guilt!

These are the main offerings of the sanctuary. Now, if all these sacrifices (and more) were needed for forgiveness and atonement under the old covenant, how much greater is Christ's sacrifice, which was "once for all" (Hebrews 9:12)? Yes, the price for our redemption is high. Romans 6:23 tells us that "the wages of sin is death," but the verse goes on to say that "the free gift of God is eternal life in Christ Jesus our Lord." The good news is that God's debt forgiveness plan is *free for you*. He already paid the price, you just have to accept the gift.

I know some people do not want charity. I know some who feel that they need to pay *something*. Well, you *can* pay for your own sin. In fact, if you do nothing, or straight up reject God's forgiveness, you will pay for it yourself—through *your* death. However, you actually have a choice. Because of Jesus' sacrifice you can choose: your death, or His substitution. If you will accept God's gift, then this is what you can expect: "And you, who were dead in your trespasses and the uncircumcision of your flesh, God made alive together with him, having forgiven us all our trespasses, by canceling the record of debt that stood against us with its legal demands. This he set aside, nailing it to the cross" (Colossians 2:13, 14). This is God's offer. If you want Him to, God will cancel the record of debt against you—*paid in full*.

Still, the full cost for our debt is not just payment (death)—there also needs to be a change of mindset and lifestyle. But praise God, He has that covered too! Notice what it says in Hebrews:

> For if the blood of goats and bulls, and the sprinkling of defiled persons with the ashes of a heifer, sanctify for the purification of the flesh, how much more will the blood

of Christ, who through the eternal Spirit offered himself without blemish to God, *purify our conscience from dead works to serve the living God.* Therefore he is the mediator of a new covenant, so that those who are called may receive the promised eternal inheritance, since a death has occurred that redeems them from the transgressions committed under the first covenant. (Hebrews 9:13–15, emphasis mine)

Yes, there is power in the blood of Christ! Because of the blood of Jesus, we can enjoy a positive relationship with God. Because of His blood, we can be at peace with God and confirm our covenant with Him. Because of His blood, we can be made right with God. Because of His blood we can be forgiven. Because of Jesus' complete sacrifice, we can be freed from the guilt of sin!

Part of the journey to having God as your King is letting Him pay off your debt. He wants to completely forgive your spiritual debt to Him and purify your choices. How does that make you feel? I am reminded of a parable that Jesus told to Simon the Pharisee after they watched a woman anoint Jesus' feet with perfume. "'A certain moneylender had two debtors. One owed five hundred denarii, and the other fifty. When they could not pay, he cancelled the debt of both. Now which of them will love him more?' Simon answered, 'The one, I suppose, for whom he cancelled the larger debt.' And he said to him, 'You have judged rightly'" (Luke 7:41–43). Yes, the more you understand how great your debt is, the more you'll love the One who forgives it. Why would you reject such an offer? Right now, before we leave Mount Sinai, will you accept God's gift and be free from the burden of sin?

"For his invisible attributes, namely, his eternal power and divine nature, have been clearly perceived, ever since the creation of the world, in the things that have been made. So they are without excuse."

ROMANS 1:20

CHAPTER 9

NO MORE EXCUSES

On a beautiful sunny day, people gathered for America's favorite pastime: baseball. The coach's eye was on one of the newest players—the rookie center fielder. The reason: he was playing terribly. The coach became worried that the team would suffer because of this young man's problems. He had already called him in twice, encouraging him to do better, but enough was enough and the coach couldn't risk it any longer. He called the rookie in one last time.

"Stay here in the dugout," the coach told him. "I'll go out there and show you how to do it." So, the coach headed out for the center field. It wasn't long before a player hit one toward him. He would finally be able to show the new kid how to play. He ran up to catch the ball. To his dismay, the ball got lost in the sun and landed at his feet. Filled with confusion and a hundred "suns" in his eyes, he allowed an infield home run.

Not long after a second ball was hit toward him. Racing to make the play, he ran right into the right fielder, injuring one of his best players. The next batter knocked a high one straight out to center field. An easy catch, the coach glanced quickly to make sure his rookie was watching and confidently raised his glove to catch the ball. Somehow, though, the ball missed his glove and hit him right between the eyes, knocking him out. A hush settled over the crowd as the paramedics rushed out to the field. They revived him and placed him on a stretcher to carry him off the field. As they passed the dugout, the coach turned to the rookie and said, "Boy, you have things so messed up out there, *no one* can play it well!"

Can you believe that? What an excuse! I've heard a few excuses in my lifetime, and even used some myself, but wow! Maybe you have given a few unbelievable excuses yourself. Of course, excuses are not exclusive to those of us in the twenty-first century. We also find them on our journey to the Promised Land. Even after the great experience at Mount Sinai, excuses abounded from the back seat. Not long after leaving the valley around the mountain, the Children of Israel had crossed the rest of the desert and were standing on the edges of their paradise: *the* Promised Land. The land where they would be truly free and God would be their King.

But before they entered, God wanted them to explore the land of Canaan. This way, they would see that it was everything that God told them it would be, and they would also know what it would take to claim it. They were instructed to choose one man from each of the twelve tribes. These twelve, then, would get further instructions from Moses. If you think about it, they were the lucky ones. They were the first to enter into Canaan. They were going to get a preview of God's promise before anyone else. What a privilege! Soon, the twelve were chosen and sent to Moses to learn what they were to do.

They did all that God, through Moses, told them to do. They explored the whole land—checking out the villages and towns, taking pictures (mental photographs, of course) of the natives, and even managing to grab a bunch of grapes on their way out. A *large* bunch of grapes. Two men had to carry the grapes between them on a pole! Imagine that today: "Hey dear, could you help me bring in the groceries? And bring a friend because I bought grapes." Finally, after forty days of exploration, they returned to the camp. As they entered the camp, people rushed up to hear their report. Excitement filled the air. What was it like? Was God right? The men showed the fruit (which should have verified God's promise alone), and started their story:

> And they told [Moses], "We came to the land to which you sent us. It flows with milk and honey, and this is its fruit. However, the people who dwell in the land are strong, and the cities are fortified and very large. And besides, we saw the descendants of Anak there. The Amalekites dwell in the land of Negeb. The Hittites, the Jebusites, and the Amorites dwell in the hill country. And the Canaanites dwell by the sea, and along the Jordan." But Caleb quieted the people before Moses and said, "Let us go up at once and occupy it, for we are well able to overcome it." (Numbers 13:27–30)

It started out as an honest report. It was everything God said it would be. It was beautiful. The land was nice. Sure, the people looked tough. It wasn't going to be easy. Then, the excuses came (not everyone shared Caleb's enthusiasm):

> Then the men who had gone up with him said, "We are not able to go up against the people, for they are stronger than we are." So they brought to the people of Israel a bad report of the land that they had spied out, saying, "The land, through which we have gone to spy it out, is a land that devours its inhabitants, and all the people that

we saw in it are of great height. And there we saw the Nephilim (the sons of Anak, who come from the Nephilim), and we seemed to ourselves like grasshoppers, and so we seemed to them." (Numbers 13:31–33)

Notice, while they gave an honest report to Moses, they deliberately sent a *bad* report throughout the people. To Moses, they said it was everything God promised it would be; to the people, they described it as the opposite of what God claimed it would be. They gave the people a report filled with excuses as to why it would be impossible. Their excuses didn't even make sense. They started to make up stories. They seemed like "grasshoppers"? *Really*? They may have known their excuses were bad, but it was the best they could come up with. Maybe it was fear that caused them to exaggerate their excuses. Most likely, it was distrust—a lack of faith in God. They wanted the land, but they did not believe God could give it to them anymore. They wanted the land, but did not trust their King. As a result, their deceptive report minimized (or completely left out) the wonderful things about the Promised Land and grossly exaggerated (to the point of lying) the obstacles they saw.

Unfortunately, the Israelites believed the exaggerations and it devastated them. Of course it would. They had heard about the wonders of the land since they left Egypt. Now, all their dreams and hopes were smashed. They even started to cry aloud. How could this be? Didn't God promise them this land? So they went to Moses and Aaron to whine, "Would that we had died in the land of Egypt! Or would that we had died in this wilderness! Why is the Lord bringing us into this land, to fall by the sword? Our wives and our little ones will become a prey. Would it not be better for us to go back to Egypt?" (Numbers 14:2, 3).

They wanted to go back? They were on the *border* of the Promised Land. They could see it with their own eyes! Yet, because of the bad report, they came up with their only solution: choose a leader to take them back to Egypt. Their minds were made up. They believed the excuses of ten men more than they believed God's promise. (This is a good example that the majority is not always right.) Joshua and Caleb were the only two men of the twelve who tried in vain to convince them to trust God. The people wouldn't listen when they were reminded about the power of God and that God was still with them. In fact, the people became so upset at Joshua and Caleb that they talked about stoning them (Numbers 14:6–10). What a strange reaction. "How dare you tell us that the land is amazing and our God is strong! How dare you tell us we can do it! We should stone you for that."

But God intervened. Again God asked, "What is it going to take to get a little faith from you? How long will you treat Me this way? Why can't you trust Me?" He confronted Israel and said, "Okay, no more excuses. What will it be? Do you want to enter the Promised Land or not?" Of course, He heard the answer in their grumbling earlier: they refused to trust in God and would rather return to slavery.

God had invited them to live in the land of Canaan and He promised to give it to them. They would live free, never to be slaves again, in this land where God would be King. It would all be theirs if they continued to trust and follow Him. Yet, according to their complaining, they were more willing to die in the desert than by the sword in Canaan. They wanted the freedom but were not willing to fight for it. They claimed they wanted God as King, but were not willing to sacrifice for it. So God gave them their wish. As a result, none of them (the complainers) would live to see the Promised Land (Numbers 14:26–35). They said He couldn't protect their children, and now only their children would survive. Instead, for forty years—one year for each of the forty days they explored the land—they would all wander in the wilderness until every last one of the unbelieving adults passed away.

Of course, once they learned this they immediately changed their minds and wanted to go into Canaan. "Okay, okay, we'll go. You were right God, it is the better thing to do. *Oopsies.* We've sinned. We know it now." But it was too late—their decision was final—no more excuses.

You might be thinking, "Well, there are no giants in my neighborhood, and I wouldn't necessarily call it a paradise, so what does this have to do with me?" Here's why this is relevant to you: on this journey you will find yourself on the edge of the Promised Land—the place where you can be truly free and have God as your King. You have had glimpses of it. It is a land of plenty, flowing with milk and honey (or as some today might prefer, soy milk and agave syrup). Better yet, it is flowing with living water! And you have been invited to live in this land right now. You don't have to wait until Jesus returns. He can be your King *today*.

Sadly, there will be some who have gone before you into a relationship with God only to return with a bad report. While everything was just as God had said it would be, for some reason, they only tell you about the difficulties and problems that they faced. The stories they present make it seem like a relationship with God is impossible, or worse yet, not worth the trouble. If someone in your life is giving you this report, understand that they are giving you a *bad report*. Actually, as we've seen in Israel's case, it is not just bad—it is deceptive. Do not believe such reports. The land where God is King *is* plentiful—it will not devour its inhabitants, but will give them a life more abundant. Yes, you will experience trials along the way. Yes, you will face large obstacles when you enter into a dependent relationship with God, but with God you will overcome them! No, it won't be easy, but God has promised to give it to you.

So, what is *your* excuse? What is keeping you from letting God reign in your life—completely? Is there something keeping you from accepting the invitation and walking forward into the

Promised Land? What excuses do you give yourself? What excuses do you give God?

Yes, some scouts have returned with rumors of giants: giant obstacles, giant trials, giant fears—anything that looms larger than you can be a giant. A giant that you will have to fight! Ten out of twelve will tell you that it is impossible—it is too much risk for so little return. So maybe you're scared to face these giants alone and you want to turn and run. But God says, "[F]ear not, for *I am with you*; be not dismayed, for *I am your God*. I will strengthen you, I will help you, I will uphold you with my righteous right hand" (Isaiah 41:10, emphasis mine). You will not enter Canaan alone. God isn't going to bring you all this way just to leave you fighting alone with your own strength. And if God is with you, then this promise is yours: "I can do all things through him who strengthens me" (Philippians 4:13). With Christ you can conquer *anything*. No giant is too big.

Yes, you will see giants. They falsely claim the land God desires to give you. You will have to face them if you want to live there. They will not be easy giants to defeat either. In fact, these giants can make you feel like nothing, but that's okay, because God is greater than any giant.

So the real question is: do you trust God? After all you have read about God's power and faithfulness in the Bible—after all you have seen around you and the blessings you have personally experienced from God—after all of this, do you trust Him?

"Well, I've been *trying* to trust God with my life." Really? I've learned that if we really want to do something we will do it; if we don't, we won't. Most often, we connect the idea of trying with things we either do not want to do, or think we cannot do. We embrace the idea of trying because if we happen to fail, we can feel good that *at least we tried*. However, that is not how dependence works. You either depend on God or you don't. You either trust Him or not. There is no middle ground. It is one way or the other.

"It's not that simple, it's not just black and white." That's the whole problem; it *is* just black and white. The Bible warns us about being spiritually lukewarm (Revelation 3:14–17). That's the gray area: the area of always "trying" but never doing. The Bible doesn't say, "I can *try to do* all things through Christ." It says, "I can *do* all things through Christ." Israel may have tried to trust God, but they didn't trust Him when it came down to the moment of truth.

Once again, you are faced with a choice on your journey: trust God and enter into the unfamiliar territory of complete dependence on Him, or make excuses and head back into the wilderness. You may be thinking, "You just don't understand my life." You're right, I don't. But God does—He knows everything about you—even the number of hairs on your head—and *He's* the One wanting to be your King.

Can you trust God? *Can* you trust Him with your family? *Can* you trust Him to protect you—physically, emotionally, and spiritually? *Can* you trust God with your life in the midst of giants? Paul says, "For his invisible attributes, namely, his eternal power and divine nature, have been clearly perceived, ever since the creation of the world, in the things that have been made. So they are without excuse" (Romans 1:20). There are no more excuses. Scripture reveals His faithfulness. Have you seen it? All of nature declares that God is amazing! Have you experienced this? All of creation proclaims that God is incredible! Have you learned this?

So here you are, in a new relationship with God, on the edge of the Promised Land. It is everything God said it would be. It is the ultimate goal of every Christian journey: living free from sin in a land where God is your King. Again, there will be trials ahead and giants to defeat if you want to inhabit the land. Yet, you do not have to fear: "Their protection is removed from them, and the Lord is with us" (Numbers 14:9). What excuse is left?

God wants to be King of your life. He is asking you to move forward *with Him* in faith. So, no more excuses. What will it be? Are you ready to enter into the wonderful unknown of God's rule or do you want to run back to the desert? Today is the day. Choose your King.

> "Now faith is the assurance of things hoped for,
> the conviction of things not seen."
>
> HEBREWS 11:1

CHAPTER 10

FAITH AT THE DEEP END

The chlorinated, crystal-clear blue water sparkled in the sun. I was standing on the edge of my great-aunt's pool. The sound of my cousins playing filled the air. I would soon be joining them, but not yet. At that moment, I was focused. I had something more important to do. I glanced once more at my feet, staring at the number painted on the pavement. I was at *the deep end*. I lifted up my head and focused on the one encouraging this whole event: my dad. He stood, arms open wide and a smile on his face, coaching me on. He's the one who had told me stories of the wonders of the deep end. He's the one who had told me how much fun the deep end could be. He's the one who had told me it would be easy. All I had to do was jump. He would catch me and keep me above the water.

My eyes were quickly drawn back to the water. It wasn't that easy for me. First, I had not been in the deep end before. Second, and much more significant, I could not swim! That is pretty important if you want to be in the deep end. Oh, I pretended to swim. You know, when your feet are touching the pool floor in the shallow end and you bend at the waist, making it *look like* you're swimming. I was pretty good at pretending when in the shallow end, but when it came to *actually* swimming, I couldn't do it.

Still, I had always wanted to go into the deep end. It did look fun. In fact, I was the one who had been asking to go in. But at that moment, I was questioning my request. Was it worth leaving the safety of the kiddie pool? At least there I knew where I stood. At least there I knew I *could* stand. I wasn't afraid of jumping. I had jumped many times into the shallow end. If my dad was standing in the shallow end I would jump without hesitation. Because I knew *I* could do it. *I* could keep my own head above the water if something went wrong.

Because something could go wrong. What if I couldn't jump far enough? What if he got distracted and missed me? Besides, the mystery of the deep end was enough to make it scary. Every time I looked at the bottom of the deep end, I saw *the drain*, and it never looked inviting. (It didn't help that I had heard many horror stories of the drain.)

Regardless, I was going to have to make a decision. I could jump into the deep end or run back to the comfort of the shallow end. If I waited too long Dad might leave, and I would miss the opportunity altogether. It was the moment of truth.

The Children of Israel stood at the edge of their own deep end—the edge of the Promised Land. They had heard the report of twelve spies: the land was good but the people were scary. Ten spies said that there was no way they could defeat the giant natives. Only two, Joshua and Caleb, said that the giants they saw were no match for God.

Israel was left with a choice: they could either enter Canaan fighting, or go back into the "comfort" of the desert. It was their moment of truth. What did they choose? As we learned already, they decided it was too risky and chose the desert. They chose the desert over the Promised Land. *Forty years* of wandering ahead—the Promised Land *behind*.

What happened? Didn't God promise the land to them? Yes, He did promise it to them, but they had forgotten something. They were at the deep end without something very important. We don't need to take a forty-year hike to find out what they were missing—Numbers 14:11 tells us: "And the LORD said to Moses, 'How long will this people despise me? And how long will they not believe in me, in spite of all the signs I have done among them?'"

They were missing faith. Somehow along the journey they stopped trusting in God. They looked toward Canaan with their own strength, not God's. It wasn't that they were afraid to fight, because they had fought before and won. Nor was it that God hadn't revealed His might to the Israelites; they had seen it many times. Yet, they still refused to depend on His power.

They started their trip with faith. Putting blood on their doorposts to survive Passover required faith. The Red Sea required faith. They started this journey depending on God. Yes, it was a bumpy road at first. But God continued to show His power so they could trust Him more. By this time on their journey, they had plenty of proof that God could give them the land—in fact, a few did believe. Sadly, after enjoying a few personal victories, the majority began to trust in their own power and judgment. They defaulted back to trusting themselves. They wanted to return to "pretend swimming." They decided to believe only in what they could see. By the time they arrived at the Promised Land only a few weeks after leaving Egypt, their faith was no longer in God. The result: they lost out on God's promise.

Of course, everyone who takes this journey with God will have a deep end to face, and it is at such deep ends that our faith, or lack of it, will be revealed. Faith has always been important on this journey. In fact, we are told that without faith it is impossible to please God (Hebrews 11:6). So, what is God asking from us?

What is faith? "Now faith is the assurance of things hoped for, the conviction of things not seen" (Hebrews 11:1).

This is what God wants from us. This is what it takes for us to please Him: for us to be *sure* of what we hope for, and *certain* of what we do not see. It is understandable that the Israelites realized their own weakness in the shadow of the legendary giants and fortified cities. There is little question that they would hear of those great obstacles and feel out-matched, because they were! But faith is seeing the victory in *God's* strength. He wasn't asking them to become stronger or wiser, He was asking them to have faith in Him. Evidence of this faith was being sure that God would give them Canaan (what they hoped for), and certain that the giants would fall (what they could not see). This is faith.

We may also see our weakness when we learn the requirements of eternal life, but faith is seeing victory in the strength of Christ. It is being confident that God will save us (what we hope for) and sure that our "giants" will be defeated (even though we cannot imagine it). It has nothing to do with our strengths or abilities either. It is all about God's strength. Faith is about depending on Him. *He* will fight. *He* will win. *He* will save us. *God* will complete what He's promised.

This is the key to the deep end: depending on God to fulfill His promises. Trusting that God not only wants us there, but will also get us there. This is God's promise to help us succeed on our journey to the land where He is our King: "I will give them a heart to know that I am the LORD, and they shall be my people and I will be their God, for they shall return to me with their whole heart" (Jeremiah 24:7). God desires this relationship with us so much that He is willing to give us a heart to know Him. God reveals why this new heart is so significant.

> And I will give them one heart, and a new spirit I will put
> within them. I will remove the heart of stone from their

flesh and give them a heart of flesh, that they may walk in my statutes and keep my rules and obey them. And *they shall be my people, and I will be their God.* (Ezekiel 11:19, 20, emphasis mine)

When He calls us to a deeper relationship with Him, He will give us everything we need for victory: a new heart—one that will love Him and follow Him. With this new heart, He becomes our God and we become His people.

This is why our faith is tested on the smaller things—so we will use our faith when we are at the deep end. Whatever our deep end is. Whether it is conquering a land, or conquering a habit; whether it is accepting His truth, or spreading His truth. It all requires faith.

Philippians 4:13 says, "I can do all things through [Christ] who strengthens me." Do you believe this? How do you interpret this passage? My pastor can do all things . . . my parents can do all things . . . *they* can do all things . . . or do you truly believe, that *you* can do all things through Christ? Understand this: if you do not believe that through Jesus you can do all things, then *you will not do anything.* God's ability to do amazing things in your life is only limited by your refusal to depend on Him. But, praise God, when you use the faith you have (no matter how little it is), Christ will make up the rest!

You see, this journey has never been about discovering or improving *our* strength or *our* abilities. It has always been about building our faith in God's abilities. The question is not "does God have the power?" It is "do I *depend* on His power?" The person who depends on God will not set a limit to what He can do—whether conquering the giants in the land, or saving the worst sinner. Because Christ died for the worst sinners, and the best sinners, so if *any* sinner believes that Christ's sacrifice is enough, they will not die, but will have everlasting life (John 3:16)!

It will not be our strength that gets us into the Promised Land. It will not be our good works, attendance at church, or any tradition we may hold onto that will result in God being King of our lives. It is only through faith in Jesus; it is fully depending on Him for everything—especially at the deep end.

This is the reality of the deep end: it is not a pretty place. You cannot pretend to swim in the deep end. The water is too deep.

Standing at the edge of the pool as a kid, I knew there was no way I could do it. I knew I would fall short.

"*Look at me.*" I lifted my head. My dad was still there with his arms open wide and a smile on his face. "Jump," he said. "I will catch you."

It was at that moment that I realized that it did not matter if I could not touch, because *my dad could*. What excuse could I have left for not jumping? So, with all the energy I could muster, I leapt into the air—*splash*—right into my father's arms.

Maybe you have found yourself at the deep end—facing the place in your spiritual walk where you cannot touch anymore. A point in your journey with God that is full of obstacles and giants that you cannot defeat and you know it—a situation that is beyond your abilities. You may feel like you are about to jump in over your head and you will have to do everything you can just to keep afloat. It may make you want to give up. Don't give up! Remember God's promise to give you a heart to know Him. Remember His promise to save you. Remember that it was God who promised you this relationship in the first place. The God who brought you here can take you the rest of the way!

But what if you fall short?

"Look at me," Jesus softly calls to you. He is still waiting. A smile is on His face. His arms are open wide. "Just jump," He says. "I'll catch you."

Don't worry if you can't swim. Don't worry if you can't jump far enough. Don't worry if you can't touch. *He can.* Just jump!

What are you waiting for? Do you want God to be King of your life? What excuse do you have left for not jumping? There is no better time than right now; there is no better day than today. Take the leap—jump into His powerful arms—choose today on whom you will depend.

"Some trust in chariots and some in horses, but we trust in the name of the LORD our God" (Psalm 20:7).

CHAPTER 11

THE WiLDERNESS EXPERiENCE

Have you ever decided not to try something only to find out how wonderful it was once it was no longer available to you? Maybe you have turned down a project at work because it seemed too difficult, only to see someone else accept it and receive the promotion you were hoping for. Or perhaps you have refused to try a new dish someone brought to potluck because it was unfamiliar, only to learn that it was delicious when you gave in and tasted a small portion of it, but there was no more left when you returned to get more.

This is probably how the Israelites felt when they learned that they would not inhabit the Promised Land. As we learned in the last chapter, they had heard the reports from the twelve spies, but the rest of the journey sounded too difficult and unfamiliar. They didn't have faith that God would give them the land, and they refused to enter. They told God that they would rather die in the wilderness than die trying to live in Canaan. As a result, God gave them their wish (Numbers 14:27–30): those old enough to make the decision that day would not be allowed to enter into Canaan. Of course, as many parents have experienced with their own children, as soon as God said they could not have it, they wanted it even more.

Nevertheless, it was too late. They could only watch as their hopes and dreams of a better life slipped away—as the Promised Land grew smaller in the rear-view mirror. I can imagine that some grew bitter toward God. He was being mean. He promised them the land. Why would He withhold it from them now? Why wouldn't He give them what they said they wanted?

According to God, "[Y]our children shall be shepherds in the wilderness forty years and shall suffer for your faithlessness, until the last of your dead bodies lies in the wilderness" (Numbers 14:33). They were going back into the wilderness because of their lack of faith and disobedience (Joshua 5:6). Instead of establishing lives inside Canaan, they were forced to live in the wilderness, just outside Canaan, for forty more years.

It would be easy to assume that this was simply a punishment for the Israelites, but their journey began in the wilderness. After leaving Egypt, they spent a few weeks in the wilderness learning about God and His law and making a covenant with Him. They experienced plenty of demonstrations of God's faithfulness and might. The problem was that their initial experience in the wilderness wasn't enough. Even though they had experienced many amazing things with God, they still didn't trust Him. So, instead of ending their trip and inhabiting the land with their King, their wilderness experience had to be extended.

If God simply wanted those who lacked obedience and faith in Him to die, why not just lead them to a strong army and let them be wiped out? Why not just smite them with His wrath right then and move on with their children? Why send them all back into the wilderness for forty years? While there is no question that part of the reason for returning to the wilderness was discipline—the consequence of their decision not to trust God—it was also about something greater.

So, what would be the purpose of an additional forty years in the wilderness—or *any* wilderness experience, for that matter? Moses explained the purpose in Deuteronomy:

> You shall remember the whole way that the LORD your God has led you these forty years in the wilderness, that he might humble you, testing you to know what was in your heart, whether you would keep his commandments or not. And he humbled you and let you hunger and fed you with manna, which you did not know, nor did your fathers know, that he might make you know that man does not live by bread alone, but man lives by every word that comes from the mouth of the LORD. (Deuteronomy 8:2, 3)

Do not miss the first point: God always had a purpose for the wilderness—He was guiding them. The wilderness was not a mistake. Even though we often describe their forty years as "wandering," God was leading the whole time. If the wilderness was just about punishment, then God would have sent them there and abandoned them. Yet, throughout the forty years, He took care of them.

Notice what the Bible says about His faithfulness during their extended journey. Moses reminded them, "The LORD your God has blessed you in all the work of your hands. He has watched over your journey through this vast wilderness. These forty years the LORD your God has been with you, and you have not lacked anything" (Deuteronomy 2:7 NIV). And in Nehemiah 9:21 we read, "Forty years you sustained them in the wilderness, and they lacked nothing. Their clothes did not wear out and their feet did not swell." Can you imagine this? Some people today can't even get through the day without their feet becoming swollen! And clothes not wearing out? What about their children? Those would be some serious hand-me-downs. Yeah, you could say that God took care of them. Why? Because, their time in the wilderness wasn't pointless. They weren't lost—God led them into the wilderness, and took care of them, because He had more to teach them (and us if we'll listen).

First, God needed to teach humility (Deuteronomy 8:2). The Children of Israel trusted in their own power and wisdom. They couldn't put their faith in God because it was still in themselves. How could they live with God as their King if they were still so great in their own minds? So they returned to the wilderness. Sadly, it would take forty years for the Israelites to truly humble themselves before God.

Too often we also come to God with our own achievements and our own teachings as proof that we are ready for the Promised Land. However, it is not the land where we will reign, it is the land where *God* reigns. And, if we want God as our King, we must take the current king or queen—ourself—off the throne. We can only learn to do this in the wilderness. It is in the wilderness that you learn your weaknesses and witness God's amazing power and great wisdom. Humbling yourself before God will not make you weaker, but will allow God to fully work in your life. God reminded Paul of this in 2 Corinthians 12:9, "My grace is sufficient for you, for my power is made perfect in weakness." God can't have perfect power in your life if you think you are already so great.

However, if you will learn to humble yourself, God promises, "He leads the humble in what is right, and teaches the humble his way" (Psalm 25:9). He also says, "For the LORD takes pleasure in his people; he adorns the humble with salvation" (Psalm 149:4). God can only teach you, lead you, and save you when you are humble. How long will you need to walk in the wilderness before you learn to be humble before God?

God also needed to teach obedience (Deuteronomy 8:2). Since the Israelites still trusted in themselves, they were not always willing to obey God. How could God be their leader if they were not willing to follow? The additional time in the wilderness was necessary as a test to see if they were ready to fully obey.

Sadly, we still tend to question God's commands and pick and choose the things we think are worthy to obey. Yet, if God is going to be the King of our lives, shouldn't we listen to and obey *everything* He says—and be "doers of the word, and not hearers only, deceiving yourselves" (James 1:22)? Don't be fooled into thinking you are safe because you listened to your favorite preacher or read from your favorite Christian author. Don't fall into the trap of believing that all you have to do is read through the Bible. What good is it for you if you hear God's Word *but do not follow it*? This is why God leads you through the wilderness: to give you many opportunities to learn to be a *doer* of His Word. He may start with smaller things (like the manna) to teach you that all of His commands are worth following. Because, how else could you prove that God is your King without obedience? As James wrote, "So also faith by itself, if it does not have works, is dead" (James 2:17).

How can you prove to God that you trust Him? How do you demonstrate that you are depending on Him? Through your complete obedience—you will *do* what He asks. Granted, in order to know what He wants you to do, you have to be listening. Doing what man tells you to do, or following church rules, does not mean you are necessarily following God (as we are learning with Israel, sometimes even the majority in a group claiming to be God's aren't following God). Following God means you will go to God for direction. Your resulting actions will reveal the reality of your faith in what He says. So, how long will you need to remain in the wilderness before you trust God enough for complete obedience?

This was all necessary so God could teach them dependency: "[T]hat he might make you know that man does not live by bread alone, but man lives by every word that comes from the mouth of the LORD" (Deuteronomy 8:3). The Israelites knew that they were no match for the inhabitants of Canaan, so they quit. If they couldn't conquer the land on their own, no one could. Yet, how could God be their King *in that land* if they wouldn't depend on Him to give it to them? In those days, the king always led his people in battle. By not trusting Him to lead, Israel revealed that He wasn't their King yet—they were still in charge of their lives. Therefore, they went back into the wilderness until the last of their self-sufficiency was gone.

This has always been a problem for humanity. From childhood, we are taught the importance of independence, so losing it is viewed as a bad thing. In fact, we have been conditioned to think that dependence on someone else is weakness. This could not be further from the truth, especially when it comes to God. The truth is, you cannot enter the Promised Land on your own.

A life with God as King requires a *dependent* relationship. How, then, can you enter into it without learning to depend on Him first? Interestingly, Jesus quoted Deuteronomy 8:3 near the end of His own wilderness experience (Matthew 4:4—this is additional proof that the wilderness isn't about punishment). His time in the wilderness solidified His full dependence on God, because it is through the toughness of the wilderness that we are reminded of our need for God. Your experience with God in the wilderness will reinforce the promise that "I can do all things through him who strengthens me" (Philippians 4:13). In fact, the point of the wilderness is to make this promise your declaration. How long, then, will you be required to remain in the wilderness until you will fully depend on God?

You see, God reveals the ultimate reason He will lead you into the wilderness: "The LORD says, 'During the forty years that I led you through the wilderness, your clothes did not wear out, nor did the sandals on your feet. You ate no bread and drank no wine or other fermented drink. *I did this so that you might know that I am the* LORD *your God*" (Deuteronomy 29:5, 6 NIV, emphasis mine). In the Hebrew language, knowledge is based on experience. This means that God's ultimate purpose for taking you into the wilderness is so you can *experience* Him even more. He leads you into, and through, the tough, barren times of your life so you can experience His power, wisdom, and grace. It is through this experience that you can learn humility, obedience, and full dependence on Him.

No, living in the wilderness is not the goal—it may be a nice place to visit, but you wouldn't want to live there. Nevertheless, if you want to live in the Promised Land, where God is truly your King, you will have to follow Him through the wilderness. How long you stay in the wilderness, though, is up to you.

"And as Moses lifted up the serpent in the wilderness, so must the Son of Man be lifted up, that whoever believes in him may have eternal life. For God so loved the world, that he gave his only Son, that whoever believes in him should not perish but have eternal life."

JOHN 3:14–16

CHAPTER 12

POISONED!

Imagine a beautiful day. The sun is shining, birds are singing, and a warm breeze flows through your hair. It is so peaceful you just want to soak it all in. And you do, until—*ouch*—you feel a sharp pain in your heel! You look down just in time to see a tail slither into the ferns. You stand there in horror as you realize that a snake has just bitten you. Old PBS specials flash through your mind and you recognize the snake as a poisonous one. Your heart races and a warm feeling washes up your leg—a warm, numbing feeling. It feels like your blood is starting to boil as a fever sets in. Your head begins to swim. A rash develops and begins to itch. This is so much worse than that time you had the flu!

You quickly dig into your backpack. You take a couple Tylenol for your fever, but even at Extra Strength how much good could they really do? You put some Cortizone-10 on your rash, which cools the itch but, honestly, the itch is the least of your worries. It dawns on you that even your faithful, daily doses of Flintstone Vitamins will be of little help.

You might feel a temporary peace as these treatments subdue the symptoms. But, as long as the poison is in you, you're still in trouble. Then a fantastic idea enters your mind, you could suck it out! You've seen it done before. To your dismay, you remember that the bite is on your heel and, well, you're not that flexible.

It becomes gravely evident: every moment this poison continues to run freely in your veins is a moment closer to your death. You don't need comfort—you need a cure. You need the antidote, and you need it now!

I'm sure it started as a beautiful day for Israel as well. They were well into their forty-year extension on their trip to Canaan, enjoying the blessings from God, when *it* happened.

> From Mount Hor they set out by the way to the Red Sea, to go around the land of Edom. And the people became impatient on the way. And the people spoke against God and against Moses, "Why have you brought us up out of Egypt to die in the wilderness? For there is no food and no water, and we loathe this worthless food." Then the LORD sent fiery serpents among the people, and they bit the people, so that many people of Israel died. (Numbers 21:4–6)

Notice that venomous snakes bit the Israelites, shortly after they sank their fangs into Moses. They suddenly turned against God and Moses and began to complain. In their impatience, they became extremely ungrateful. They even claimed God's miracle of manna was worthless! They basically told God, "We hate your blessings." They had a curse of poison in their heart—which led to being bit. They had been poisoned, but not by snakes. Still, it took the snakes to illustrate the danger they were in.

Unfortunately, after being freed from the curse of slavery to sin, we can still find ourselves poisoned on our journey. After we have experienced the blessings and mercy of God we can become bitter and angry toward Him, even to the point of hating His blessings. Indeed, in the midst of our journey with God, we can find still ourselves bitten by a terrible snake.

It's a poisonous snake too. Its venom spreads fast, taking effect in our lives: Poisonous Passions flow in us, boiling our blood, causing us to turn against the things of God. A Fanatical Fever grows, keeping us always "hot under the collar." A Religious Rash develops, and we scratch everywhere on the surface, while ignoring the real problem. Its symptoms are reminiscent of how we were before Christ found us:

> Now the works of the flesh are evident: sexual immorality, impurity, sensuality, idolatry, sorcery, enmity, strife, jealousy, fits of anger, rivalries, dissensions, divisions, envy, drunkenness, orgies, and things like these. I warn you, as I warned you before, that those who do such things will not inherit the kingdom of God. (Galatians 5:19–21)

This is not the kind of list the people of God want used to describe them. We are rescued from sin to be different. Yet, this poison can return to our lives even after being saved from it.

The scary thing is that this poison is not only deadly but it is also contagious, and it spreads quickly. Granted, it will not continue forever. Eventually, it will end—one way or another—because either we'll get the cure, or we'll succumb to the poison. Regardless of how long our life displays the symptoms, if the poison remains in us, we will eventually die. So, if we want to live, we can't wait. We don't need comfort, and we don't need "warm and fuzzy" pep talks, we need the cure!

Sadly, some will dig into their religious backpack and rely only on the advice of the "spiritual" experts of man—concerned only about the symptoms. You may take your "tithe-n-all" to church each week to ease your fanatical fever, but even with extra giving it doesn't seem to help. Or maybe you will wash in the baptismal tank ten times hoping to cure your religious rash. Sure the cool water feels great, but without an internal change you only come up wet. Yet, these things will only subdue the symptoms; they can't cure the problem. Sooner or later, you'll realize that even your faithful daily doses of [insert your favorite Christian author/ speaker here] vitamins won't have much affect. These are not life-giving activities, but only (and barely) life support. You still have the poison in you. So what do you do?

Let's look at the solution God offered to Israel. The Israelites quickly learned that they couldn't get rid of the poison through their own efforts. Many also realized that they were wrong—that they shouldn't have attacked Moses and God. So they called out to God and asked for help. When Moses prayed on behalf of the people, God answered with an antidote—a way out, but only one. "And the LORD said to Moses, 'Make a fiery serpent and set it on a pole, and everyone who is bitten, when he sees it, shall live.' So Moses made a bronze serpent and set it on a pole. And if a serpent bit anyone, he would look at the bronze serpent and live" (Numbers 21:8, 9).

It is interesting that the Israelites asked God to remove the serpents, yet He didn't. Instead of removing the serpents, He gave them an antidote. The serpents would remain with them. They would be a continual reminder of the results of allowing sin back into their lives should they, once again, forget how wonderful God is. While God did not remove the snakes, He did remove their death sentence; though the serpents still lived, they had a cure.

The Israelites had the chance to become whole again. It was extremely simple: look and live. Take it or leave it. Live or die. Sadly, the Bible doesn't say everyone looked. It just says that if they looked they lived. With such an easy solution, why would someone *not* look? Could it have been pride? How about self-sufficiency? Perhaps some of them, proud of how far they had come in life, tried to keep pressing on with the symptoms, accepting them as a natural part of getting older—grumbling all the way to the grave. I can also imagine that there were others who, although they believed that the bronze serpent was not necessarily a bad idea, felt more confident of the new, 100% vegan, gluten-free, and non-GMO ointment they just purchased from the Wilderness Shopping Network. They would rely on their own remedies, easing their symptoms, giving themselves "life support."

Of course, there is a difference between life support and life. Satan encourages life support; God wants you to have *life*. Satan argues, "You will not surely die, *right now*." God says, "You do not have to die, *ever*." (I like God's version better! Don't you?) It was Israel's choice, but *only* if they looked at the bronze serpent did they live. Was it too simple? No. Those who trusted in God's plan looked and lived.

Our choice is no different: life support or life abundant. Just as God provided an antidote for Israel, He offers us a cure as well today. "And as Moses lifted up the serpent in the wilderness, so must the Son of Man be lifted up, that whoever believes in him may have eternal life" (John 3:14, 15). Some people argue that this is too simple—there must be more that we should have to do. Yet, the Bible tells us it is that simple, and that "*whoever believes in him* may have eternal life." We often spend too much time helping ourselves by trying to ease our symptoms, while ignoring the simplicity of God's solution. We must not forget that if we get rid of the poison, the symptoms will be gone too! Jesus wasn't lifted up to ease our symptoms—or make us comfortable—but to completely cure us from the poison forever.

Like the serpent in the desert, Jesus was lifted up for all to be saved. Therefore, to be cured of this poison, our choice is as easy as the one for the Israelites: we have to look. The cure for a mid-journey poisoning is to go back to the cross and witness the sacrifice made on your behalf again, so you can believe in Him again. Yes, you have already been to the foot of the cross at the beginning of the journey, but that doesn't mean you never look again. In fact, if we stay away from the cross too long, we might forget about how bad sin is. Because it is there at the cross—the last moments of Christ's life—that we are reminded of the true cost of our anger, bitterness, and discontentment toward each other and toward God. It is there that we are also reminded of the true nature of the amazing God who loves us sacrificially. It is at the cross that we are reminded not only of the severity of the poison but also of the power of the cure.

A lady once told me that she took two aspirin every morning. Curious, I asked her why. She told me it was to prevent her from getting a headache during the day. Although I'm not sure of its medical merit, I think this advice works well in this case: spend time at the cross every day and you can prevent the poison from entering back into your life.

Nevertheless, do not be surprised that even in the middle of your Christian journey you may find yourself infused with Satan's venom. He is always ready to attack and will not give up. In fact, as I have experienced, Satan seems to fight harder the closer I try to get to God. He uses many different ways to cause us to become bitter and selfish, and his poison is still very deadly.

And, just like in the desert, only Christ can cure us. Only He can purge us of the poison. Without Jesus there is no cure, no healing, no life. But there's a good reason. Galatians 3:13 says, "Christ redeemed us from the curse of the law by becoming a curse for us—for it is written, 'Cursed is everyone who is hanged on a tree.'" He can cure us because He became the curse—the Antidote —for us. He does not *have* the antidote; He *is* the Antidote. He *is* life. *As long as Jesus fills our lives, the poison cannot.*

There was another beautiful day. A couple was out for a walk in their garden. The birds were singing and the sun was shining. Then, the woman felt a sharp pain. Almost instantly, the man, too, felt the fangs. In horror, they realized that a snake—a deadly, deceptive snake—had bitten them. It did not take long for them to realize the snake was poisonous. A warm, numbing feeling of right and wrong washed up their legs. It hadn't seemed harmful before. Of course, they had been warned about how poisonous it was, and yet they still played with it. Now their lives had become infected—and contagious—and headed for death.

Sadly, this was only the beginning; God warned them that the snake would continue to bite. And it did. God did not remove the serpent; He did not make it so the Enemy could not deceive anymore. No, that sly serpent would bite the heels of many for a long time, but not forever. Its head would be crushed; an antidote would be made; a cure would be found.

Yes, somewhere on this Christian journey you may find yourself poisoned—getting resentful, angry, even ungrateful toward God and each other—but there is a cure! God has given us an Antidote: Jesus. But you cannot delay. Without Christ, the Antidote, you cannot live. It doesn't matter who you are. It doesn't matter how bad you know you are or how good you think you are. The promise in John 3:16 says, "For God so loved the world, that he gave his only Son, that whoever believes in him should not perish* but have eternal life." In the Israelite camp, whoever looked upon the bronze snake was cured. Likewise, *whoever* believes in Jesus will be saved! Whoever. Are you a "whoever"? If so, this promise is for you!

Understand, though, it is not simply believing that Jesus lived and died a long time ago. Even the demons believe that. To believe in Jesus is to depend on Him for your salvation. To know that Jesus didn't just die, but that He died *for you*. He took your place

---

* This phrase contains the strongest negation possible in the Greek language. "Should not perish" does not portray the full impact of it. A better translation would be, "it is impossible to perish." In other words, when you choose to believe and trust fully in Jesus, it is impossible that you will perish, but you are guaranteed eternal life!

in death to sin. He paid for your sin. He redeemed you from the curse. So, when you return to the cross and behold His sacrifice, remember that He did all of that, endured all of that, because *He loves you.* Believing this means that sin does not own you anymore —you are God's!

Friend, it was on the cross that Christ redeemed you from the curse. Because of this, He can remove the venom threatening to take you out. But it's up to you to let Him. You have to choose. Will you look? Will you look to the One who gave His life for you? Will you settle for life support, or will you accept His offer of life abundant? Jesus was lifted up on that old rugged cross so you can look upon Him and be cured. So, "Today, if you hear his voice, do not harden your hearts" (Psalm 95:7). Look to Jesus and live!

"And you shall eat and be full, and you shall bless the Lord your God
for the good land he has given you. Take care lest you
forget the Lord your God…"

DEUTERONOMY 8:10, 11

CHAPTER 13

SETTiNG UP STONES

The Israelites stood at the side of the Jordan River, having just crossed into Canaan, and they were listening to their next instructions. It may have been hard to pay attention. They were on the *other* side of the river. They were actually standing *in* the Promised Land—the land where they would live with God as their King. Of course, they also knew that they would soon face tremendous obstacles and great battles. But before any battles, before facing any enemies, and even before the fall of Jericho, God instructed them to gather stones. It was a strange request: select twelve stones, one for each tribe in Israel, and bring them to Joshua. Not just any stones either—they were to be collected from the middle of the river, where the priests were still standing, *on dry ground*, with the Ark of God.

After the stones were brought up from the river, they were taken to their campsite, and Joshua set them up as an altar. The stones were not selected for souvenirs; they were meant for something much greater. According to Joshua, the altar of stones would remain at this place so that in the future, when their children would ask what those stones meant, they could tell them the miraculous story of God parting the Jordan River. The stones were to be "a memorial forever" (Joshua 4:7) for Israel. God did not want them to forget what He did for them that day. Furthermore, these stones were to serve as a reminder, "so that all the peoples of the earth may know that the hand of the Lord is mighty, that you may fear the Lord your God forever" (verse 24). Much like memorials established today, this altar was to remind anyone else who might pass that way that the Lord is mighty. It was also meant to keep Israel in awe of God.

We might wonder why such a reminder would be necessary. At that moment, Israel was on a spiritual high. They had just crossed the Jordan River on dry ground (during flood season even). How could they ever forget that? Looking toward Jericho after such an incredible experience, they were filled with complete trust in God. Their faith in God was at an all-time high. Of course, they had just come out of the wilderness with forty years of experiences that proved that God was faithful. With God leading, they would soon move through Canaan and conquer it. Life couldn't be better. Sure, they would slip a few times in their obedience, but for the most part they would hold on to God and continue to remember how He brought them safely through the wilderness. Unfortunately, their memories would eventually fade.

God knew that they would need something to keep them from forgetting His power and majesty. They would need regular reminders to fear the Lord (we still need such reminders today too). As Moses had urged them before, "You shall remember that you were a slave in the land of Egypt, and the Lord your God redeemed you" (Deuteronomy 15:15). We usually tell people to "remember" things when we believe that they will forget. So, these stones were meant to remind them where they started (in slavery), how God delivered them, and how far He had brought them (to Canaan). This is important because we can easily forget what God has done for us if we forget where we started. The truth is: we would still be slaves to sin if it wasn't for God!

It was not just for the individual to remember either. God's plan was that the stones would cause their children to ask questions, giving the parents the opportunity to teach them of His greatness. Notice the reason David gave:

> He established a testimony in Jacob and appointed a law in Israel, which he commanded our fathers to teach to their children, that the next generation might know them, the children yet unborn, and arise and tell them to their children, so that they should set their hope in God and not forget the works of God, but keep his commandments; and that they should not be like their fathers, a stubborn and rebellious generation, a generation whose heart was not steadfast, whose spirit was not faithful to God. (Psalm 78:5–8)

God wanted Israel to teach their children about Him so they would learn to trust in God and end the heritage left by their forefathers of forgetting Him. Thus, these stone memorials were meant to be reminders *and* offer teaching opportunities. At each memorial, the Children of Israel were given the chance to pass down to their children the wonders of following a faithful God.

One would think that such magnificent stories of the miracles and the power of God would easily be passed down and taught throughout future generations. However, not many years after the land of Canaan was conquered, Israel had already forgotten. Tragically, just a couple generations later, their grandchildren were worshipping pagan gods.

It is not surprising though. We see the same thing today. I had the privilege of serving as a youth pastor several years ago. During that time, I frequently heard from the youth that they would hear their parents, or other adults, talking about how great God is, but their actions never matched their words. Adults may not know this (though we should), but the youth are watching us! They hear what we say and watch what we do. They are often witnesses to the hypocrisy of modern "religiosity"—we talk the talk but don't walk the walk. At church we may say that God is trustworthy, but in the real world we won't trust God with our lives. Is this what we want to pass down to our children? Like the Israelites, we have the opportunity to teach our youth about the greatness of God—not just by our words, but also by our actions. We have been given the responsibility of sharing the stories of God's faithfulness in our lives to our children "so they should set their hope in God and not forget the works of God."

The Israelites learned the hard way that life is not better when they forget God. As He said, "Know and see that it is evil and bitter for you to forsake the LORD your God; the fear of me is not in you, declares the Lord God of hosts" (Jeremiah 2:19). Yes, evil and bitterness invade our lives when we stop thinking about God. Israel experienced this evil and bitterness far too often.

Unfortunately, we are no better. We are prone to such forgetfulness as well. Too often we claim to be "Christian" yet forget about Christ in our daily lives. We can go about the "business of Heaven" while neglecting the power and guidance that comes from Heaven. We are also guilty of forgetting the power of God in our lives and no longer fearing Him. Sadly, this is the religious experience for far too many these days—and with it comes the evil and bitterness of forgetting God.

How can people so easily forget what God has done in their lives? How can the "people of God" fail to remember the greatness of their God? Actually, as history shows, it is quite easy. Have you ever found yourself at the end of a day, a week, or a year, and had a hard time remembering God's blessings in your life?

Not long ago, I was talking with one of my childhood friends and he mentioned one of his favorite memories of something we did together. Yet, no matter how many details he gave, I could not recall that moment. In fact, he spoke about several occasions that I couldn't remember. I felt like a terrible friend! Then, a moment later during our "trip down memory lane," I brought up one of my favorite moments and *he* did not remember it. However, during our conversation, I learned that he recalled many of those stories because he had written them down or had retold them several times. I realized that I was not alone in my forgetfulness. We tend to forget important things because we don't write them down or share them with others.

Interestingly, even when we establish memorials we can still forget. Moses warned the Israelites about something that would greatly challenge their memories in spite of the memorials. In Deuteronomy 8:11–14, he revealed the situation that would cause their forgetfulness:

> Take care lest you forget the LORD your God by not keeping his commandments and his rules and his statutes, which I command you today, lest, when you have eaten and are full and have built good houses and live in them, and when your herds and flocks multiply and your silver and gold is multiplied and all that you have is multiplied, then your heart be lifted up, and you forget the LORD your God, who brought you out of the land of Egypt, out of the house of slavery.

According to Moses, the leading cause of forgetting what God has done in our lives is *a life of peace and personal success.* It doesn't take a great detective to figure that out though. This is the experience of everyone following God. It is easier to remember God when life is a struggle. When we are at the end of our rope, it is so much easier to remember to look up. But what about when everything seems to be going our way? The greatest threat to our memory of God's majesty is a nice and easy life. Again, just look around. What happens during major disasters? People flock to religion. In moments of crisis, people suddenly remember God. After the great tragedy of 9/11, churches were packed. Large groups of people were looking for God. However, a few months later, when everything went back to normal, many of those same people stopped coming. When life was bad, they looked to God; when life was good, they forgot about Him. Sadly, this can be true for all of us if we are not careful.

Success is not the problem, though; it is just a catalyst to take our eyes off of God. There's no doubt that, while Israel followed God, success was in their future. He promised them success and peace in a land of plenty. These are God's plans for all those who follow Him: "For I know the plans I have for you, declares the LORD, plans for [peace] and not for evil, to give you a future and a hope" (Jeremiah 29:11). He wants to give us these things and so much more, He just doesn't want these things to take us away from focusing on Him. Truly, the greatest danger in success is that we can begin to think that we are doing so well because of our own efforts (Deuteronomy 8:17). Because of this, Moses counseled Israel to always praise the Lord for *everything* they received, otherwise they would become proud and forget God. As scripture and history reveal, though, the Israelites did not follow Moses' advice.

We might shake our heads at Israel over this, but we are not any better. Moses' counsel is for all who choose to follow God, because when you decide to start this journey your life *will* change—usually for the better. When God's blessings are poured out, you will experience greater peace and success in your life than ever before. Remember God's promise: the final destination of your journey to make Him King of your life is success and peace in the land of plenty. However, because of this, you are also in danger of this prosperity causing you to forget about God.

Sadly, in times of peace and plenty it is easy to forget about God rather than to praise Him for His blessings. When we have reached the "bottom" it feels necessary to look up, but what about when we reach the "top"—the times of peace? We call on God when we are sick, but do we remember to praise Him when we wake up well? We seek God when we have nothing, but what about when we seem to have all we need?

This will be a constant issue for us as we enter into, and get comfortable in, the Promised Land. It is revealed in the mindset of the Laodiceans, mentioned in Revelation: "For you say, I am rich, I have prospered, I need nothing . . ." (Revelation 3:17). Sadly, this describes much of modern Christianity. It is easy to believe that we are rich today. We have great churches and cathedrals, extravagant worship services with incredible musical talent, and a warm caring atmosphere. Yet, something is not right. With all that we *have*, there is still something definitely *missing*. A closer look at the problem of Laodicea reveals that Jesus is outside the church (Revelation 3:20). What happened to the Israelites so long ago has reoccurred in twenty-first century churches: we have forgotten our God.

If you have this feeling of emptiness in your spiritual life, it is a strong indicator that you need to visit memorials from your past. You might need to be reminded of the greatness of your God. Heed the warning of the angel of Revelation: "Fear God and give him glory, because the hour of his judgment has come, and worship him who made heaven and earth, the sea and the springs of water" (Revelation 14:7). Yes, you might need to learn to be in awe of Jesus again. You might need to make God the focus of your worship again. You might need to remind yourself where you started, how God has delivered you, and how far He has brought you. So you must return to the stones.

What stones have you set up? What have you done to make sure you remember what God has done for you? Have you done anything? No, you won't need to go out to the nearest river and collect several stones, one for each tribe in your family. Today, your memorials will look different. You could write in a journal or make a scrapbook of God's blessings in your life. You could write a blog, a poem, or a song. Leave yourself a ton of Post-It notes, tie a string on your finger, or make regular trips to the place where those special moments happened. It doesn't matter how you choose to do it—just do it. Don't let circumstances cause you to forget your God. Set up your stones so you will remember to "cling to him and to serve him with all your heart and with all your soul" (Joshua 22:5). Return to those memorials and meditate on the greatness of God. Then, share it! The greatest way to visit and remember your memorials is to share those memories with someone else (especially the youth).

Can't think of any recent experience? It is possible that you have not set up any stones lately. Unfortunately, if you do not acknowledge His blessings, you will not remember them. If you cannot think of anything recent, go back further. You may have to go back to when you first heard the gospel—when you first looked upon your Savior hanging on the cross. Go back to the first time you felt God working in your life. Who cares about how ancient the stones are? Revisit those memories and remind yourself of the love of God.

Perhaps you are just starting this journey. Maybe you never thought to look for God's blessings in your life. You do not have to wait until you are standing in Canaan to establish a memorial. The miracle of the Red Sea happened at the beginning of the journey for Israel. I can assure you, it would always stand as a memorial for the Israelites. They did not need to erect an altar of stones to remember; the sea itself would remind them. If you have never taken count of your blessings, then stop right now—

wherever you are on your journey—and set up your first memorial. Acknowledge God's leading in your life to get you to this place.

Friend, whether you are taking your first steps inside the Promise Land or you have been an inhabitant for a while, you have another great opportunity to establish a memorial. Whether you are setting up stones for the first time or you have created many "memory" altars in your life, you can never have too many reminders about the power and majesty of God. They're not just a pile of stones; do not underestimate the importance of setting them up. They can remind you about where God found you, rescued you, and where He is taking you. They can remind you why you fell in love with Him in the first place. And revisiting these ancient stones gives you another chance to relive those moments with God. They give you another chance to grow in Him—another chance to place more trust in Him.

As you enter into the Promised Land—the land where you will experience the best God desires to give you—take care, lest in all of this you forget the Lord your God.

"...I will give the inhabitants of the land into your hand, and you shall drive them out before you. You shall make no covenant with them and their gods. They shall not dwell in your land, lest they make you sin against me; for if you serve their gods, it will surely be a snare to you."

EXODUS 23:31–33

CHAPTER 14

THE FALL OF CANAAN

There was once a spider who built a beautiful web in an old house. He kept it clean and shiny so that flies would be attracted to it. The minute he got a "customer" he would clean up after it so the other flies would not get suspicious.

Then one day a fairly intelligent fly came buzzing by the clean spiderweb. Old Man Spider called out, "Come in and sit." But the fairly intelligent fly said, "No sir, I don't see any other flies in your house, and I am not going in alone!"

Soon, the fly saw on the floor below him a large crowd of flies dancing around on a piece of brown paper. He was delighted! He was not afraid if lots of flies were doing it so he came in for a landing.

Just before he landed, a bee zoomed by, saying, "Don't land there, stupid. That's flypaper!" But the fairly intelligent fly shouted back, "Don't be silly. Those flies are dancing. There's a big crowd there. Everybody's doing it. That many flies can't be wrong!" Well, you know what happened. He landed and was stuck with the other flies "dancing" to free themselves. What does it profit a fly if he escapes the web only to end up in the glue?*

Have you ever experienced something like this? Some times we want to do what everyone else is doing so badly that we end up in a mess. We might avoid danger when no one else is involved, but like the fly, we easily fall into a trap because "everyone is doing it." Whether it is through the "encouragement" of some friends or the awkwardness of being the only one not participating, peer pressure is a major part of our lives. While some pressure we face may be beneficial, peer pressure is most often associated with bad influence. Scripture warns us to avoid harmful role models. Take this example of a warning from Paul: "Do not be deceived: 'Bad company ruins good morals'" (1 Corinthians 15:33). Regardless of our age or spiritual strength, over time these negative influences will adversely affect our walk with the Lord. Of course, Satan is determined to pull us back into sin and wreck our lives, and he often uses destructive influences to accomplish his goal. This is why an important moment in our journey with God involves recognizing and removing the power of such negative examples.

Wait a minute. We are standing in the Promised Land. We've exited the bus because we've made it—we're at the destination printed on our ticket. The journey's finished, right? Not quite. Unfortunately, too often, as soon as we feel that we've "arrived" with God, we stop the journey. Yet, there's still something *very* important to do. We will understand what remains if we continue observing Israel's experience.

Israel had left their former life of wandering in the desert and were marching toward Jericho, the first battle in their conquest of Canaan. The sudden change of activity may seem strange to us. Sure, they had fought some battles getting here, but

---

* Chuck Swindoll, "Peer Pressure," in *Day by Day* (Nashville: Thomas Nelson Publishers, 2000), https://www.insight.org/resources/daily-devotional/individual/peer-pressure.

they were already inside the land God promised to give them. Why, if this was *their* land, were they marching against this fortified city? While we may question the reasoning behind their latest instructions, the Israelites knew they would have to fight to conquer the land. This is why they were so scared forty years earlier (see chapters 9 and 10). Back then, they couldn't see victory against the giants of the land; now, they marched into Canaan confident in their God.

They knew what they had to do—more specifically, they knew what God *would do through them*. Moses had previously explained this important part of their journey:

> When the Lord your God brings you into the land that you are entering to take possession of it, and *clears away many nations before you*, the Hittites, the Girgashites, the Amorites, the Canaanites, the Perizzites, the Hivites, and the Jebusites, seven nations more numerous and mightier than you, and *when the Lord your God gives them over to you, and you defeat them, then you must devote them to complete destruction*. You shall make no covenant with them and show no mercy to them. (Deuteronomy 7:1, 2, emphasis mine)

Yes, God would fight for them (as He promised) and give them victory over the nations, but they also had something to do: they were to devote the defeated nations to complete destruction. They were not to show any mercy. Seems a bit harsh, doesn't it? It doesn't sound like the same loving, merciful, and patient God we've been following. It doesn't sound like the God who called us to respect life as a part of our covenantal relationship with Him. In fact, this mandate for Israel is often used against the character of God. Such a command makes it easy to argue, "How could God be loving if He demanded the destruction of the Canaanites?"

While it is easy to question God's love because of such a command, we cannot let this conflicting statement cancel out everything we've already learned about God. Yes, many who do not already know God will question His love, but by this point in our journey there should be no question in our hearts that He is loving because we've personally experienced it. In fact, God isn't just loving—*He is love* (1 John 4:7, 8). Therefore, the question isn't, how could He, but rather, why would He?

Right around the time the Israelites were camping by Mount Sinai, God revealed the battle plan for the future fall of Canaan, as well as the reason why.

> And I will set your border from the Red Sea to the Sea of the Philistines, and from the wilderness to the Euphrates, for I will give the inhabitants of the land into your hand, and you shall drive them out before you. *You shall make no covenant with them and their gods. They shall not dwell in your land, lest they make you sin against me; for if you serve their gods, it will surely be a snare to you.* (Exodus 23:31–33, emphasis mine)

According to God, He wanted the Israelites to drive out the other inhabitants from Canaan because of their religion. The gods and traditions of the pagan nations would easily entrap them again—they were too similar to what God rescued them from in Egypt (see Leviticus 18:3). Even within the borders of the Promised Land—yes, *especially* here—our adversary attempts to ensnare us into slavery once again. Enticing us with ideas we used to cherish in our old life is a favorite tactic of our enemy. It is particularly dangerous at this point in the journey, because this is where many let their guard down. It can be easy to assume that once we have made it to the land where God is King, His Lordship will just . . . well, *happen*. But it doesn't. There are still many things that will try to destroy our relationship with Him. If we are not aware of the spiritual ambush that is waiting, we will be easily defeated.

Even the newly formed Christian church, during the time of the Apostles, struggled with the trap of false worship and beliefs. In his letter to the church in Galatia, Paul said of their struggle, "I am astonished that you are so quickly deserting him who called you in the grace of Christ and are turning to a different gospel" (Galatians 1:6). Later in the letter, he revealed the reason for their abandonment of the gospel: "You were running well. Who hindered you from obeying the truth? This persuasion is not from him who calls you. A little leaven leavens the whole lump" (Galatians 5:7–9). They weren't alone in needing the warning either because he gave similar counsel to the church in Corinth (1 Corinthians 5:6).

You see, the spiritual battle isn't over just because we enter into a trusting relationship with God. There will still be influences in our lives that will attempt to draw us back into our old life. In God's warning to the Israelites, we can see His concern was about their relationship with Him. He knew that the powerful lure of the Canaanite gods could tear them away from Him. Thus, if Israel truly desired God to be their King, they had to fight to remove anything that would compete for their loyalties.

In fact, a great example that God's order was not about the complete destruction of the people is the story of Rahab (see Joshua 2). Although God's instructions were to destroy Jericho and its inhabitants (Joshua 6:21), Rahab and her family were spared (Joshua 6:17, 23). If this command was simply genocide, God would not have spared them. Yet, He did. What made the difference? Although most, if not all, of the people of Jericho had heard the stories of Israel's God, only Rahab was in awe of Him as a result (Joshua 2:9–11). Her dawning respect for Him caused her to be kind to the Israelites—the only way she knew to show kindness to their God. Her faith in God resulted in the salvation of her and her family from the destruction.

In addition, the fact that Jericho was a fortified city means that it was most likely a military outpost. If so, its inhabitants would have been leaders, military, and other support (Rahab would have been considered "support" for the military). The ordinary citizen would have lived *outside* the city. As a matter of fact, there is no archaeological evidence of civilian populations living inside Jericho.[†] Therefore, since the order specified killing those in the city, those living outside the walls would not have been part of the destruction. While it does not mean that all of the citizens outside the city were spared, recognizing the details of the order, along with the story of Rahab, provides reasonable evidence that other Canaanite families could be saved from destruction.

In other words, the conquest of Canaan was more like the refining process of silver or gold in the fire. When these metals are mined from the ground, they are often mixed with many other elements. In order to make the metals pure, they must be refined —submitting the metals to high temperatures to remove any impurities. Only after this process is complete can the metals become useful for their intended purpose. Canaan needed to be refined. It was never simply about the people. It wasn't a military conquest meant to subdue nations who stood in the way of Israel inhabiting the land. Devoting the nations of Canaan to destruction was about ridding the land from the impurities of its false worship. People and animals were only involved in the destruction because while God was removing the false gods and traditions from the land, anyone or anything that continued to hold onto or be connected to them would be wiped out too. God made it very clear, "[I]t is because of the wickedness of these nations that the LORD is driving them out before you" (Deuteronomy 9:4).

---

† Paul Copan, *Is God a Moral Monster?* (Grand Rapids: Baker Books, 2010), ebook.

Sometimes we forget who the people of Canaan were. They were the descendants of Canaan, the grandson of Noah and the son of Ham. Most of the people listed living in the area—the Amorites, Girgashites, Hivites, and Jebusites—were from the children of Canaan. The Bible tells us that Canaan was cursed to serve his brothers (Genesis 9:25, 26). Being cursed makes it easy to assume that neither he, nor his children, had any hope of being godly—as if they were doomed to destruction. However, he was also called to be a servant of God (Genesis 9:26). While some suggest that the Canaanites probably didn't know any better, Paul reminds us, "For what can be known about God is plain to them, because God has shown it to them. For his invisible attributes, namely, his eternal power and divine nature, have been clearly perceived, ever since the creation of the world, in the things that have been made. So they are without excuse" (Romans 1:19, 20). The people of Canaan had known about God. They were called to be His people as well. Everything about God was available for them to know, so they were without excuse. They *should* have known God. They *should* have been servants of God. Yet, somehow, as time passed, they grew away from Him.

The nations of Canaan were living examples of what happens when people reject God. By the time Israel had crossed into the land, the Canaanites had completely abandoned God and chased after pagan ideas. They embraced terrible atrocities—all in the name of religion. They even offered their children as a sacrifice —a *burnt* offering—to the god Molech (Jeremiah 32:35). It isn't surprising that God called their lifestyle "unclean," and their actions "abominations" (Leviticus 18:24–30). He warned the Israelites to never practice these abominable customs, for if they did, the land would "vomit you out when you make it unclean, as it vomited out the nation that was before you" (Leviticus 18:28). Those appalling traditions, and all who practiced them, could not remain in the land.

These atrocities are what God desired to purge from Canaan. If they remained, Israel would be lured away from their relationship with Him. Again, if God had only wanted the land completely cleared of the people, He would not have given such instructions as these:

> [W]hen the LORD your God gives them over to you, and you defeat them, then you must devote them to complete destruction. You shall *make no covenant with them* and show no mercy to them. *You shall not intermarry with them*, giving your daughters to their sons or taking their daughters for your sons, for they would turn away your sons from following me, to serve other gods. Then the anger of the LORD would be kindled against you, and he would destroy you quickly. *But thus shall you deal with them: you shall break down their altars and dash in pieces their pillars and chop down their Asherim and burn their carved images with fire.* For you are a people holy to the LORD your God. The LORD your God has chosen you to be a people for his treasured possession, out of all the peoples who are on the face of the earth. (Deuteronomy 7:2–6, emphasis mine)

Yes, Israel was to devote them to complete destruction—the destruction of their altars, idols, and pagan customs. As long as these practices were allowed to remain, they would only be a stumbling block for Israel.

You see, Satan has long succeeded in convincing mankind that the experience of disobedience is better than obedience (see Genesis 3). *A lot* of people have been convinced of this, which makes it even more appealing: *everyone* is doing it. It is very telling how great this temptation is by simply looking at the journey of Israel. They always seemed to find it difficult to worship God, but were quickly enticed to worship the gods of the other nations. Much later in their history, they easily accepted and obeyed the strange pagan traditions—including sacrificing their children to the gods—but found it a burden to obey God's commands. Even worse, they eventually adopted all of the pagan practices while claiming to worship God.‡

It is important to know the enemy's schemes, not to cause you to abandon the journey, but so that you will be prepared for the traps that lay ahead. Satan hasn't given up just because you entered into the Promised Land. Actually, now that you've made it, he will work *harder* to destroy your relationship with God. Do not give up now! Do not let everything that has happened on this journey so far be for nothing. Fight for your relationship!

But what if Canaan doesn't fall? What if you do not obey God's command and fight to keep loyal to Him? Once again, our answer is found in Israel's experience. They didn't follow God's instructions—they made covenants with the Canaanites and did not remove their religion. As a result, the nations remained among them and, according to God, "[T]hey shall become thorns in your sides, and their gods shall be a snare to you" (Judges 2:3). If Canaan doesn't fall, you gain thorns and snares. In other words, if Canaan doesn't fall, your efforts to stay true to God will become much more difficult and you will risk losing everything.

This is why *your* Canaan *must* fall. On your journey with God, you must remove anything that will compete for your loyalty to Him. Anything that may entice you back into your old life must go. It may not be as easy to identify as it was for the Israelites. You may have to take a long, hard look at your life. Is there any-thing from your "old life of sin" that you still cherish? A bad habit

---

‡ This is another reason God wanted the religion of the Canaanites gone. Deuteronomy 12:2–4 tells the Israelites to destroy the pagan places of worship, altars, and idols. He didn't even want the locations of false worship used again because, "You shall not worship the LORD your God in that way."

or unhealthy tradition, perhaps? Maybe a friend who tries to get you to [*insert any lifestyle activity you left*] again, "like old times." Maybe it's a movie, a website, a nightclub, a game, certain music, or social media that causes you to long for Egypt. It may even be the desire for personal achievement, like the need for notoriety or the pursuit of perfection. Whatever it is, it needs to go. You must devote it to complete destruction.

Yes, it is harsh, but it is necessary. God has already set you free from sin. Do you want to go back to that miserable life? What do you gain by escaping the web only to be caught in the glue? Think about it: why would you want to keep something that would only hurt your relationship with God? Besides, is that person who would tempt you to leave God truly a friend? Is it worth keeping that "friend," cherished activity, or the unful-fillable desire for personal achievement around if it only makes it more difficult to stay true to God? Does something destructive suddenly become safe simply because everyone is doing it? The answer to all of these is no. Therefore, you can trust that when God tells you to remove these things, He is not asking you to give up anything that is beneficial; rather, He is trying to protect you from the pain of falling back into slavery.

This may be the hardest part of the journey. Just when you think you have left slavery far behind, it rears its ugly head. Everything you've grown to hate about your old life is waiting to attract you all over again. It doesn't seem fair, and it isn't, because Satan doesn't play fair. But you are not going into this blind. God has warned you of these traps, and as you have already learned, God will fight the battles for you (see chapter 2 if you need a reminder). So, take a step of faith toward Jericho. Ask God to reveal the influences of Canaan in your life that need to fall and then devote them to complete destruction. Do not compromise. What do you have to lose, besides thorns and snares?

"I call heaven and earth to witness against you today, that I have
set before you life and death, blessing and curse. Therefore choose life,
that you and your offspring may live, loving the LORD your God,
obeying his voice, and holding fast to him, for he is your life..."

DEUTERONOMY 30:19, 20

CHAPTER 15

A GOOD TiME FOR A REViVAL

You've done it. You've made it to the Promised Land and
God is your King. It is possible that some time has
passed and you have become settled into your new life as
God's child. Everything about your spiritual life has been amazing.
Bible study is exciting and fresh. Your prayer time is cherished and
intimate. You couldn't be happier with your relationship with
God. Everything seems to be rainbows and roses. Then, something happens. Maybe a habit you never confronted from your
past comes back to haunt you. Perhaps you simply fall into a rut
and your spiritual life becomes nothing more than a bland
routine. Whatever the case, you slip. Yes, you still live in the land,
but God doesn't seem to be your King anymore. Somehow, in
spite of all you have done to prevent this, you still find yourself
separated from God.

If this describes your current spiritual life, you are not alone.
Unfortunately, this happens to every one of us who starts this
journey with God. As with any relationship, you will have your

ups and downs. We should know by now that Satan will do whatever he can to make our relationship with God fail. Therefore,
we cannot quit when things get tough. We must not give up if we
tend to drift away. If this relationship is worth the journey, we
must also do whatever we can to help it succeed. Yes, even when
you have a healthy relationship with God there will be times of
trouble. Fortunately, there's one more lesson we can learn from
Israel's story to help us in this struggle.

You see, Israel's experience in Canaan wasn't flawless either.
They did not obey God's commands to remove the religion of the
Canaanites, and it became a constant snare for them. As a result,
from the book of Judges onward, they frequently slipped in and
out of their covenant with God. It didn't help that they eventually
chose to have a king over them (to be like the other nations),
replacing God as their king. They were fairly stable during the first
three kings (Saul, David, and Solomon) but the nation ultimately
split into two—which resulted in the divided kingdoms of Israel
and Judah. It went downhill from there. While some of the kings
of Israel and Judah were godly men who guided God's people back
to a relationship with God, most of them followed the examples
of idolatrous nations and became very wicked and led the people
further away.

Even after the counsel of great prophets such as Elijah and
Elisha, it wasn't long before the nation of Israel was taken captive
by the king of Assyria as a result of their increased wickedness.
The northern kingdom of Israel was out of the picture now and
only the southern kingdom of Judah remained. Although Judah
was known for having better kings, its people were only a step
behind Israel in their wickedness. Just one generation after Israel's
captivity, Judah's kings were just as wicked as Israel's. In fact, the
Bible says that Manasseh led the people to do *more* evil than even
the pagan nations God chased out of Canaan earlier (2 Chronicles
33:9). Although Manasseh had a late conversion, it was too late to

impact his son Amon. Two years into Amon's wicked reign, his own officials joined in a conspiracy against him and assassinated him in his own palace. Soon after, the people of the land killed everyone who was involved in the plot against the king. In the end, they established Amon's son as king—his name was Josiah, and he was eight years old.

Talk about a plot twist. The people of Judah placed the eight-year-old son of a very wicked man on the throne. In what reality would *that* be a good idea? Of course, it's not so ridiculous if you think about it from their view. By bringing Josiah in so young, they could train him to be the king they had always dreamed of having. In essence, they could *create* their own king. It sounded like a good plan, but how did it turn out?

The Bible says, "[H]e did what was right in the eyes of the LORD, and walked in the ways of David his father; and he did not turn aside to the right hand or to the left. For in the eighth year of his reign, while he was yet a boy, he began to seek the God of David his father" (2 Chronicles 34:2, 3).* He was already a good kid, but in his eighth year on the throne, when he was *sixteen*, he began to seek God. As a teenager, in the dysfunctional land of Judah, the desire to know God grew in his heart. Let that sink in. In spite of being surrounded by the idolatry, wickedness, and influential adults who rejected God and left obedience behind, this young man decided he wanted to know God. The adults in Josiah's day may have thought they could do a great job training their king, but this young man decided to be trained by God. It is a good thing too. This desire, and resulting relationship, made a huge impact on his life and his leadership.

---

* As was noted, Josiah was Amon's son (see 2 Chronicles 33:25). Yet, these verses refer to David as his father. This is commonly used in the descriptions of the godly kings of Israel and Judah. However, if the king was wicked and rebellious against God, their actual father was referenced (e.g, in 2 Chronicles 33:22, it says of the wicked King Amon, "And he did what was evil in the sight of the LORD, as Manasseh his father had done.")

Four years later, by the age of twenty (his twelfth year on the throne), he was already active in God's work (2 Chronicles 34:3). He made it a priority to purify the land of all its idols. At an age when it is so much easier to "fit in" with the local fad, he actually cleared the fad out of his life *and* his land. Can you picture it? This young king was *taking on* the local entertainment. People may have watched as he tore down the local party shops. Some probably cheered when he took down certain seedy places that had a bad reputation. I'm sure the cheering stopped, though, when he demolished other seedy places they had come to love. Then, he made it personal, knocking down statues of celebrated evil and replicas of gods. Anything that was worshiped above God was removed. Just like the original mandate in the conquest of Canaan, Josiah refused to allow anything to remain that could be a negative influence on him or his people.†

Then, by age twenty-six, when he had finished freeing the land of false worship, he began working on the church by repairing the sanctuary (2 Chronicles 34:8). Typically, when we think of "working on" the church, we think of purifying it by dropping a few members. *We would be a much better church if so-and-so was not here. They bring our perfection quota down.* I have heard it said that before you start discussing dropping imperfect members, you need to take a look in the mirror—you might be the first to go! This is not what Josiah had in mind, but he was not expecting what happened either. "While they were bringing out the money that had been brought into the house of the LORD, Hilkiah the priest found the Book of the Law of the LORD given through Moses" (2 Chronicles 34:14).

This may not seem like a big deal, but consider what happened. While they were fulfilling their duties for the project to repair the

---

† I'm not suggesting that you put down this book, head to your local bar, and tear it down. Josiah was king of Judah, and therefore Judah was his life. By making him king, the people gave him permission to change things. Besides, before you can worry about someone else's idols, you need to clean out the idols in your own life.

temple, they *found* scrolls that contained the Book of the Law given by Moses. Again, think about this: as they were cleaning out *the church*, the *priest* happened upon some *lost* scrolls. He didn't know they were there! This is kind of like going through stuff packed away in the attic and suddenly finding something that had been missing for a while—*Hey! That's where my favorite Furby was!* How long had these scrolls been missing? How would you feel if the pastor of your church, or the church itself, hadn't seen a Bible in years? It is not surprising that, during Israel's spiritual decline, God's Word went missing. It should also not be a surprise then that, when it is time to purify His people, God will lead them back to His Word—to His law—often forgotten and lost.

Immediately, they reported the newly found scrolls to the king. As they read the scrolls to Josiah, he tore his clothes. Why?

> Go, inquire of the LORD for me and for those who are left in Israel and in Judah, concerning the words of the book that has been found. For great is the wrath of the LORD that is poured out on us, because our fathers have not kept the word of the LORD, to do according to all that is written in this book. (2 Chronicles 34:21)

They knew about the Ten Commandments. They most likely knew about the laws in Leviticus and Exodus as well. So what was it that made him react this way? Many believe that the portion read to him was from Deuteronomy. If you've ever read it, you can imagine why. If you haven't, I'll show you why.

Deuteronomy was Moses' final effort to instill God's law to the Children of Israel. This was his moment to remind them of their agreement with God. This is what he said:

> And if you faithfully obey the voice of the LORD your God, being careful to do all his commandments that I command

you today, the LORD your God will set you high above all the nations of the earth. And all these blessings shall come upon you and overtake you, if you obey the LORD your God. (Deuteronomy 28:1, 2)

Was Judah high above all nations? Not even close! Nearly every neighboring nation was licking their lips, ready to devour them. However, Moses followed that statement with the blessings God wanted to pour out on them if they would just listen to and follow Him (Deuteronomy 28:3–13). It is a long list—and I encourage you to read through it—but here is a brief summary. They would be blessed wherever they lived, whether in the city or in the country. Whatever they put their hands to do for work would be blessed. Whether they were coming or going, their trip would be blessed. If an enemy tried to attack, their enemy would be defeated and be scattered as they fled. The blessings God would pour out on them would be seen by all of the other nations—it would be evident that they were God's chosen people, holy to Him. In fact, because of His great blessings, the other nations would be in awe of them. They would prosper with children and with cattle (i.e., their livelihood). God would even open up the treasuries of heaven to bless them, so much so, in fact, that they would be able to lend to others and never have to borrow. Then, Moses concluded with this declaration: "And the LORD will make you the head and not the tail, and you shall only go up and not down, if you obey the commandments of the LORD your God, which I command you today, being careful to do them" (Deuteronomy 28:13).

If Josiah heard this, he was no doubt shocked. Judah wasn't experiencing *any* of these blessings. Of course, if he heard this, he must have heard what came next. Moses further explained, "[I]f you will not obey the voice of the Lord your God or be careful to do all his commandments and his statutes that I command you today, *then all these curses shall come upon you and overtake you*" (Deuteronomy 28:15, emphasis mine). While blessings followed faithfulness to God, curses were the inevitable consequences of refusing to obey God (these are not punishments, but rather, the natural outcome of life outside of God).

Again, the list of curses is long—*very* long; in fact, it is more than twice as long as the list of blessings (Deuteronomy 28:15–44). Most of the curses are basically just the opposite of the blessings: cursed wherever you live, cursed in your work, and cursed in your travels. There are similar contrasts with their enemies: the Israelites would be defeated and scattered by their enemies. However, there are a few additions. They would become confused and frustrated in all that they did until they were destroyed. Sicknesses would stick to them until they were consumed. They would be afflicted with wasting diseases, with fevers and inflammation, and with drought, rot, and decay. They would be plagued with sores that could not be healed. Their minds would be cursed, leading to madness and confusion. Social issues would increase —they would be oppressed and robbed continually with no one to come to their aid. Possibly the worst thing for them was left for last: they and their king would be taken captive by other nations, where they would become "a horror, a proverb, and a byword among all the peoples where the LORD will lead you away" (Deuteronomy 28:37). If they rejected God's counsel and rebelled against Him, the traveler in their midst would be better off than them—even the temporary passerby would become their master.

You want to talk about eye opening! Imagine if you were Josiah hearing this for the first time. If ever he wondered why all this bad stuff was happening, he received his answer with this. Israel had definitely strayed away from God and broken their covenant with Him. Josiah's reform was a good start, but they needed something more—they needed a revival!

Naturally, we would love to assume that the blessings describe what we deserve, but they often don't. If we are honest, we'll have to admit that we are often like Israel, even in the bad stuff. We like the promises and blessings that come with being God's people, but we neglect the responsibility. We are often distracted by "the other nations" and have also wandered from God. We frequently fall short of *full* obedience, and as a result, break our covenant with Him. We might not like to admit it, but we relapse just like Israel and Judah. Like them, after we have gone astray, we also need more than just reform—we need a revival.

This was the very purpose of what Moses wrote in the book of Deuteronomy. Even as Israel was about to enter into Canaan, they needed such a revival. God had to remind them, once again, where He originally found them and restore to their memories all He had done for them in the wilderness (Deuteronomy 29:1–7). In light of this reminder, He called them all to stand before Him, "so that you may enter into the sworn covenant of the LORD your God, which the LORD your God is making with you today, that he may establish you today as his people, and that he may be your God, as he promised you, and as he swore to your fathers, to Abraham, to Isaac, and to Jacob" (Deuteronomy 29:12, 13).

This is the revival—a renewal of their covenant agreement with Him: they are His people and He is their God. It is evident by this event outside of Canaan that renewing the covenantal agreement must happen often. How often? That depends on how much distraction is around. Let's consider a relationship among mankind that is similar: marriage. Although a couple may not officially renew their vows often (or ever), how often should they remind themselves that they are married? Let's say that the husband works with a beautiful, smart woman who purposely strokes his ego, or that the wife corresponds with an intelligent, charming man she met online who intentionally sends flirtatious notes. With such distractions (and there are infinitely more than these), would it be important that they frequently remembered that they are married? Of course! I'm guessing most would say they need to do it every day. Likewise, renewing our commitment to God should be done daily. With every "god" of this world fighting to win our affection away from God, why wouldn't we?

Israel's example (all of the curses realized in their lives) shows us what happens if we don't renew our commitment to God daily. Still, there is hope! Moses told them that when they strayed, which they would, God would restore them when they came back (see Deuteronomy 30:1–3). If they would admit that they fell away from God and return to Him to renew their covenant, this is what God promised to do:

And *the* Lord *your God will circumcise your heart and the heart of your offspring, so that you will love the* Lord *your God with all your heart and with all your soul, that you may live.* And the Lord your God will put all these curses on your foes and enemies who persecuted you. And you shall again obey the voice of the Lord and keep all his commandments that I command you today. The Lord your God will make you abundantly prosperous in all the work of your hand, in the fruit of your womb and in the fruit of your cattle and in the fruit of your ground. For the Lord will *again* take delight in prospering you, as he took delight in your fathers, when you obey the voice of the Lord your God, to keep his commandments and his statutes that are written in this Book of the Law, *when you turn to the* Lord *your God with all your heart and with all your soul.* (Deuteronomy 30:6–10, emphasis mine)

Isn't God awesome? Even though Israel would leave God many times, whenever they returned to Him, He would always accept them back. This promise is true for us as well. No matter how many times we abandon God, if we will return to Him with our whole heart, He will gladly accept us back. The truth is, every one of us will stray away from Jesus at some point in our walk with Him (even more than once). It's not *if*, but *when*. However, like the father in the parable of the Prodigal Son, God is *waiting* for us to return, and the moment we turn to come back, He runs *to us* to welcome us home.

Maybe you think that you have gone too far away, or left too many times, and that God wouldn't want you back. Friend, it may be hard to believe, but God—the Creator of the universe— *wants* to be in a relationship with you. He will do everything possible to have that relationship with you—He showed us that at the cross—so He doesn't have to think twice about accepting you back if you wish to return. As Jesus said, "whoever comes to me I will never cast out" (John 6:37).

Yes, you might have messed up. Yes, you might have broken up with God. You might have even had some harsh words with Him, or snuck behind His back and cheated on Him with your past life, but He'll still accept you back. It's not too late to come home. No matter where your decisions have taken you, you are still His, and He is still your God. Don't worry about how filthy you might be. God says, "Come now, let us reason together . . . though your sins are like scarlet, they shall be as white as snow; though they are red like crimson, they shall become like wool" (Isaiah 1:18). He can forgive you and cleanse you (1 John 1:9) if you just come back to Him.

Before they entered Canaan, Moses called the people to recommit to God. It is possible that Josiah used the same call to revival for the revival in his day:

See, I have set before you today life and good, death and evil. If you obey the commandments of the LORD your God that I command you today, *by loving the LORD your*

God, by walking in his ways, and by keeping his commandments and his statutes and his rules, then you shall live and multiply, and the LORD your God will bless you in the land that you are entering to take possession of it. . . . I call heaven and earth to witness against you today, that I have set before you life and death, blessing and curse. *Therefore choose life,* that you and your offspring may live, loving the LORD your God, obeying his voice and holding fast to him, for he is your life . . . . (Deuteronomy 30:15, 16, 19, 20, emphasis mine)

This is your call too. A fully dependent, personal relationship with God is what this journey is about. It is the reason you started following God in the first place. If you want to keep your relationship strong, you will need a revival regularly as well. It doesn't need to be scheduled; it is always a good time for a revival. In fact, you can renew your covenant with God right now. Have you slipped and need to restore your relationship with Him? Choose life: return to the God who loves you with an everlasting love! Is your relationship pretty good for the moment, but you want to strengthen it and reconfirm your commitment? Choose life: keep walking with the God who has freed you and blessed you beyond measure. No matter where you are on the journey currently, you have been shown the blessings that spring from a life with God and the evils that result from a life without God. Therefore, *choose* life. Today, in this moment, and every day hereafter, *choose* to love God, obey Him, and hold onto Him with all your strength, for He *is* your life.

For further studies on this and other topics,
visit the author's blog at:
www.overcominglaodicea.org

Other books available by Bill Kasper:

"Follow Me."

Two of the most powerful and life-changing words to come from Jesus. Those who would accept this invitation would be known as His disciples. Today, Christians still place a lot of emphasis on the importance of becoming a disciple. But what is a disciple? What does a disciple do? What does discipleship look like in real life? Too often, the answers to these questions are assumed to be understood. As a result, although we make the choice to be a disciple, whether recently or years ago, we may not have a clue about what we are supposed to be doing. It doesn't have to be this way. God's Word is very clear and open about discipleship. Maybe you need to start with the basics—Discipleship 101. Perhaps you would like a refresher course. In this book, using Jesus' teachings and stories from the Bible, Pastor Bill leads you to a better understanding of what it means to be a disciple and how you can live as a follower of Jesus.

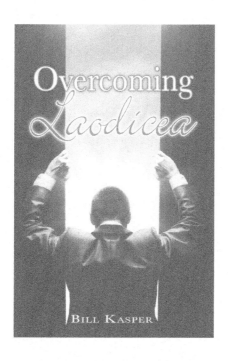

Knock, knock.

**"I know your works: you are neither cold nor hot . . .
You are lukewarm." Revelation 3:15, 16**

We have the truth, fancy buildings, and elaborate worship services. We have prayer meetings, Bible studies, and community outreach programs. Yet something is still missing. In spite of our religious appearance, many of our churches no longer resemble the church written about in the book of Acts. Many Christians today are not easily distinguishable from the world. We may go through the motions, but our heart isn't in it. This is what happens when our "Christianity" is neither hot nor cold, but lukewarm. How could God's people get to this point? In this book, Pastor Bill examines the letter to the church of Laodicea, found in the book of Revelation, to reveal the true source of lukewarm spirituality as well as how we can overcome this predicament and have a renewed passion for God.

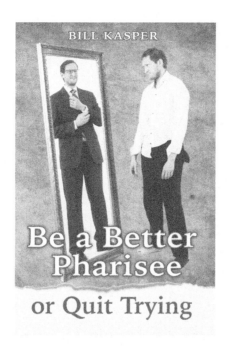

BILL KASPER

Be a Better Pharisee

or Quit Trying

**Every good work you have done
towards gaining eternal life is worthless.
Your Christian best will never be good enough.**

Your reaction towards those statements might mimic those of the Israelites in Jesus' day. It was the basic idea Jesus was expressing when He said, *"unless your righteousness surpasses that of the Pharisees and the teachers of the law, you will certainly not enter the kingdom of heaven"* (Matthew 5:20). In that one statement by Jesus, all of their preconceived ideas of God and salvation were put into question. They saw the Pharisees as their models of holiness which few, if any, could ever dream of equaling. If their best wasn't good enough, who *can* be saved? Why even try? Of course, what if Jesus wanted us to quit trying? What if Jesus has something better in mind for us?

In this book, Pastor Bill takes a hard look at the teachings, traditions and lifestyle of the Biblical Pharisees and why they experienced rebuke from Jesus so often. Filled with stories and practical application, this book reveals not only the modern issue of the Pharisaical mentality but also Jesus' solution.

Made in the USA
Middletown, DE
09 December 2020